FOOTBALL
A BEGINNER'S GUIDE

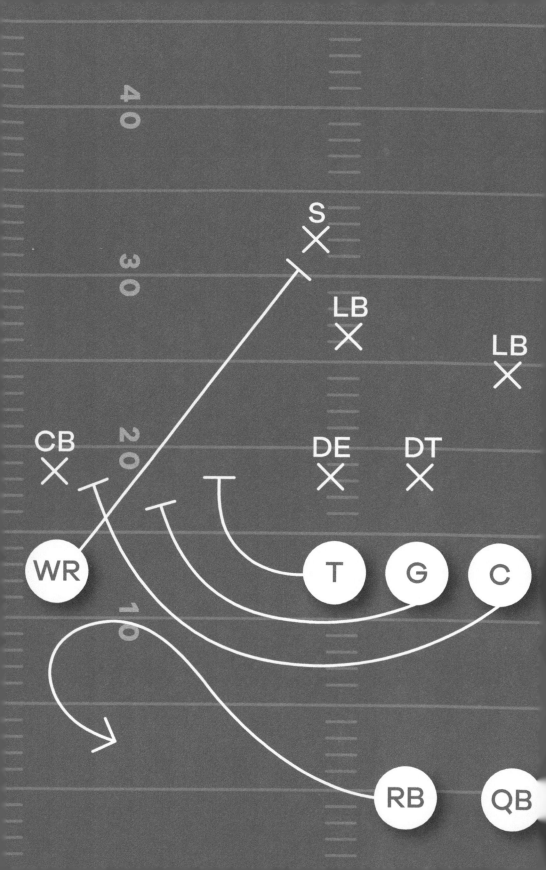

FOOTBALL

A BEGINNER'S GUIDE

LEARN THE BASICS TO WATCH AND ENJOY THE GAME

JERRETT HOLLOWAY AND RAFAEL THOMAS

ROCKRIDGE
PRESS

First Rockridge Press trade paperback edition 2022

Rockridge Press and the Rockridge Press logo are trademarks or registered trademarks of Callisto Media Inc. and/or its affiliates in the United States and other countries and may not be used without written permission.

For general information on our other products and services, please contact our Customer Care Department within the United States at (866) 744-2665, or outside the United States at (510) 253-0500.

Paperback ISBN: 978-1-63807-678-0
eBook ISBN: 978-1-63878-508-8

Manufactured in the United States of America

Interior and Cover Designer: Angela Navarra
Art Producer: Melissa Malinowsky
Editors: Rebecca Markley and Rachelle Cihonski
Production Editor: Matthew Burnett
Production Manager: Jose Olivera

Illustrations © 2022 Pelin Kahraman, pp. ii, x, xi, 70, 77, 78, 79, 80, 81, 85, 86, 87, 88, 89; JP Waldron/Cal Sport Media/Alamy, p. cover; Jonathan Bachman/Reuters/Alamy, p. xvi; Dean Bertoncelj/Shutterstock.com, pp. vi, 7; Anton Kravtcov/Alamy, p. 9; Lucy Nicholson/Reuters/Alamy, pp. 19, 20; Jeff Haynes/Reuters/Alamy, p. 21; MediaPunch Inc/Alamy, pp. 22, 23; Kirby Lee/Alamy, p. 24; Duncan Williams/CSM/Alamy, p. 27; Mike Blake/Reuters/Alamy, pp. 36, 37; Ian Halperin/UPI/Alamy, p. 40; Hum Images/Alamy, p. 46; CMS/Alamy, p. 56; Allan Dranberg/Cal Sport Media/Alamy, p. 59; Eric Canha/CSM/Alamy, p. 65; Jevone Moore/CSM/Alamy, p. 69; Ed Wagner, Jr./Chicago Tribune/TNS/Alamy, p. 92; BC/TS/Bruce Gordon/UPI/Alamy, p. 98; Mike De Sisti/Milwaukee Journal Sentinel/MCT/Alamy, p. 100; The Bloomingtonian/Alamy, p. 109.

10 9 8 7 6 5 4 3 2 1

To my nieces and nephew. Always follow your dreams and never give up.

—Jerrett

I dedicate this book to my mother, Loreda (may she rest in peace), and father, Ralph. Thank you both for allowing me to find my own voice and take my own path; I hope all your hard work has finally paid off.

—Rafael

CONTENTS

INTRODUCTION

"ARE YOU READY FOR SOME FOOTBALL?" We are Jerrett and Rafael, and we are always ready for some football. We hope you are ready too and are really glad that you've chosen this book to help you out. We are two football enthusiasts that will be guiding you through this book and America's game. We both love football and have spent years in front of our televisions watching, learning, and studying the game, including singing along with Hank William's famous opening song for decades of Monday Night Football (it's definitely worth looking up).

As avid football nerds who have played the game and have cheered for the Philadelphia Eagles and the New York Jets for our lifetimes, we want to share everything we know to turn you into a football fan and, at a minimum, help you if you just want to learn more about football. Believe me, we know how confusing football can seem at first. We remember when first watching as a kid, we thought it was nothing but players tackling each other and yelling at the referee. Eventually, we learned there is so much more that goes into the game and it isn't hard to learn at all.

With this book you will learn the history of football, the objective of football, how football is played, and the amazing players the game has seen throughout the years. There is so much to share, and we're certain you'll become a true fan by the end (pick your favorite team carefully)! Once you're done with this book, you can go out and impress all your football-watching friends with your newfound knowledge. Truthfully, you may even end up teaching them a thing or two.

Assuming you won't read the whole book in the course of two days, we've provided a Football Primer that gives a bare bones explanation of the game. While you won't learn enough to talk shop with your football fan friends, the next few pages will guide you through a game, and will provide a necessary foundation for the rest of the book. We've also bolded and defined important terms that you will see throughout the book (or in the glossary on page 111) and may hear while watching a game.

But enough of us getting you excited to read this book—dive in and see for yourself.

FOOTBALL PRIMER:
WATCH A GAME TODAY

THE FIELD

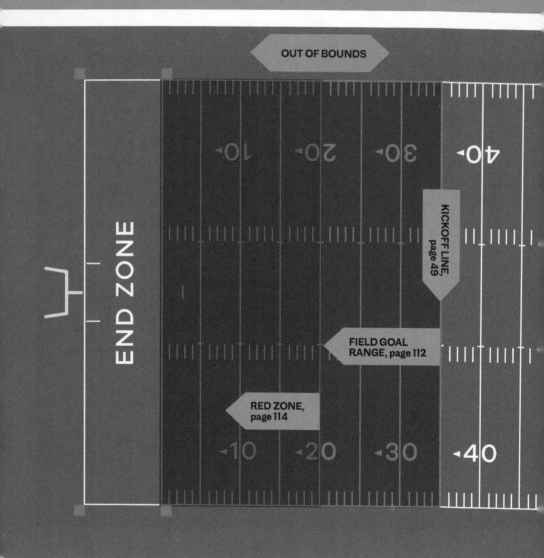

OUT OF BOUNDS

END ZONE

KICKOFF LINE, page 49

FIELD GOAL RANGE, page 112

RED ZONE, page 114

10 20 30 40

10 20 30 40

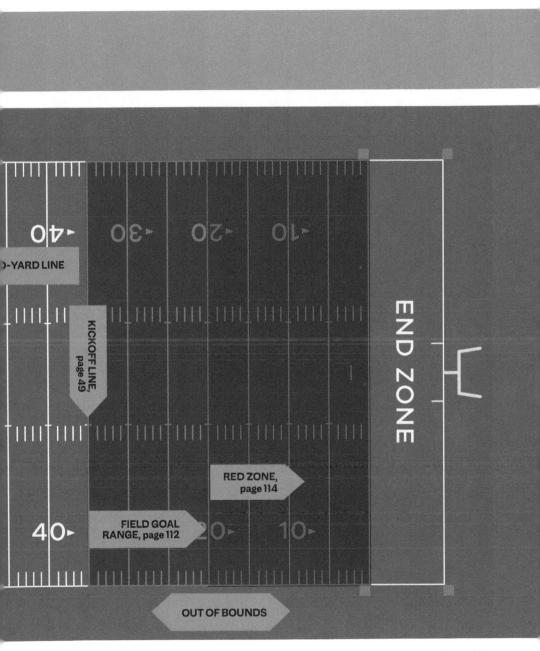

O 40 ▶

0-YARD LINE

OƐ 30

KICKOFF LINE, page 49

O2 20

RED ZONE, page 114

OL 10

END ZONE

40 ▶

FIELD GOAL RANGE, page 112

20 ▶

10 ▶

OUT OF BOUNDS

THE BASICS

A football game is made of two halves, each with two 15-minute quarters. Each team can call up to three timeouts per half, and each half has an automatic timeout at the two-minute mark before the end of the half, dubbed the **two-minute warning**.

THE COIN TOSS: A referee holds a coin toss and the team that wins can choose to **receive** the ball (meaning they are on **offense** and have the first chance to score) or **defer** and instead receive the ball first in the second half, thus giving the ball to the other team first to start the game.

THE KICKOFF: The kicker of the team not receiving the ball first kicks the ball downfield from the kickoff line. The **receivers** of the offensive **special teams** are downfield, hoping to catch the ball and run it as far as possible toward the **end zone** at the other end of the field. They can also signal a **fair catch**, which allows them to catch the ball without a chance of being tackled, but they cannot run to gain more yards if they choose this option. If the ball is kicked into or behind the end zone, the ball is automatically placed at the 25-yard line. While uncommon, if the kicker kicks the football out of bounds on either side of the field, the offense chooses between getting the ball where it went out of bounds or at the 40-yard line.

OFFENSIVE PLAY: The offense will have four **downs**, or chances, to gain 10 yards from the initial **line of scrimmage** (the starting point for each new set of downs) by throwing or running the football. For example, if a team runs the ball on first down and gains two yards from the line of scrimmage, they must now make an additional eight yards on their next three tries. (The next play would be referred to by the commentators as a "second and eight," as in, it's now second down and the team needs eight more yards before it gets a new set of downs.) The line of scrimmage moves to the spot where the previous play ended.

If they make 10 yards or more, they get a new set of four downs and the current line of scrimmage is used as the starting point for the next 10-yard requirement for a first down. This repeats until the offense scores or doesn't get at least 10 yards in its four downs, or until they reach the end zone.

Most times, if a team has not made 10 yards after the third down, on fourth down they will attempt a field goal if within field goal range, or punt the ball so that the other team starts their offensive play farther downfield.

Occasionally, a team may decide to spend their fourth down attempting to make the 10 yards. If they are unsuccessful, the other team takes over the ball wherever it is on the field.

If the offense scores either a **touchdown** or a field goal, the scoring team's kicker will then kickoff to the opposing team's receivers so that their team's offense can take over and try to score.

SCORING: A team can score by making a touchdown for six points (with the option to kick for an **extra point** or run a play on the field for a **two-point conversion**) or a field goal for three points.

DEFENSIVE PLAY: While the offense is trying to score, the defense is trying to prevent them from scoring by keeping them from gaining yards. It can do this in any number of ways, including **sacking** (**tackling**) the quarterback behind the line of scrimmage, **blocking**, preventing catches, and tackling running backs or receivers before they gain yards.

While trying to stop the offense from gaining yards, the defense can also work to get the ball back for its team by forcing a **fumble** (dropped ball) and recovering the ball, or by an **interception** (when a defensive player catches the ball thrown by the opposing quarterback). This is called a **turnover**. In both cases, the defense on the field will have the opportunity to run toward its end zone and potentially score.

TWO-MINUTE WARNING: Playing the clock is an important aspect of football, and this automatic timeout at the end of the second quarter allows teams to develop a strategy to approach the final scoring opportunities of the half.

HALFTIME: This is a 12-minute break between halves. The teams retreat to their locker rooms and work to make adjustments to their game plan for a more successful second half. This is also when epic speeches are made in the locker room to rally the team.

SECOND HALF: Played much the same as the first half, though each team has likely altered their strategy to approach their opponent differently based on the first half results. There is another two-minute warning at the end of the fourth quarter.

THINGS TO KNOW:

1. On the last play of each quarter, the play will continue until completion, even if time runs out on the clock.

2. Penalties play a major role in football. Check out the guide on page 64 to help you understand them.

3. The clock continues to run after each play, except on an incomplete pass and **change of possession**, until the two-minute warning before halftime and five minutes remaining in the fourth quarter (see page 53). After those minute marks, the clock will stop if players go out of bounds on a running play or a successful pass completion. **Clock management** also plays a major role in football as teams try to control how much time remains especially when time starts to wind down in the first half and at the end of the game.

AMERICAN FOOTBALL FUNDAMENTALS

In this chapter, you learn about the history of football, the objective of football, and the season structure of the National Football League (NFL). If you skipped the Football Primer in the introduction of the book (page x), we'd recommend you read that before getting into the chapters. Trust us, even if you don't fully grasp every concept, the exposure to the terms and ideas presented there will help make everything click as you read through.

A BRIEF HISTORY OF AMERICAN FOOTBALL

Many consider professional football to be America's greatest sport. From its humble beginnings to becoming the most popular and coveted championship in all of sports, American football is and has been entertainment worth watching and talking about.

Although professional football reigns supreme, the game started with college teams at two New Jersey universities—Rutgers and Princeton—playing the first organized game. The rules weren't officially penned until 1892, when Walter Camp took on the project of putting them to paper. Camp himself was a college football player at Yale University before becoming a sportswriter and author, and used rugby, one of the most popular games of his era, as the basis for how football should be played. Even today, American football bears a resemblance to how rugby is played.

As America grew, so too did the game of football. When national broadcasts on television started airing every game in the 1960s, the game and the emerging media proved a perfect match. Through the 1970s and '80s, the dynasties of the Pittsburgh Steelers and San Francisco 49ers gave fans teams to root for or against as they watched legendary players perform every season. The '90s saw a resurrection of "America's Team," the Dallas Cowboys, and the 2000s welcomed the longest-running dynasty of the New England Patriots. Along the way, the National Football League surpassed Major League Baseball as the country's most popular sport. More people watch football every week during the season than any other television show. That includes not only other sporting events, but every other show that is on television, cable television, and shows that are streamed. The NFL's championship game is watched more than any other event of the year. The national camaraderie built from shared experiences of cheering for teams and players and against rivals bonds the fan bases to their teams, and solidifies the NFL's position of top sport in the country. The popularity of American football has also even spread to other countries with a few games held in London and Mexico each year.

Thanks to the growth of football at the pro level, high school and college games became more popular, with National Collegiate Athletic Association (NCAA) football now the country's second-most popular sport. This growth has also led to women's leagues, with the Women's Football League Association now fielding 20 teams across the country.

OBJECT OF THE GAME

The object of football is simple: outscore your opponent. This is done with an offense that is designed to score points (we will explain how points are scored later in the book), and a defense designed to stop the opposing team's offense from scoring. There is also a group of players on special teams, made up of a kicker along with select players from the offense and defense, who may also score points for their team, most often through kicking plays.

The offense tries to score by running or passing the football on each play and moving down the field toward the **goal line** or end zone, where a touchdown or field goal can provide points. The defense has its own players tasked with stopping the offense from advancing the football and can sometimes take **possession** of the ball for their own team, through an interception or by causing a fumble and recovering the ball. Defensive players may score points for their team if they can return one of these turnovers to their end zone for a touchdown. When this occurs, the momentum and eventual outcome of the football game can change dramatically.

As a new follower of football, you may notice that it is a game of significant physical contact, a unique feature compared to other sports. The players' uniforms are specially designed to limit the amount of injury despite the hard hits. Injuries do still occur though and these can take players out of games and change the dynamics of a single game or a whole season for a team. Every player needs to be ready to step in to play at any time.

TEAMS

Every NFL team has a 53-player roster each week of the regular season. From there, 46 players are chosen to be on the active roster for each game, meaning the remaining seven are not eligible to play. From those active players, there will be offensive and defensive players, as well as backups for most positions. There will also be specialized players on the roster, like kickers and punters, who only take the field for specific plays. For each play, one team will have 11 offensive players on the field, and the other team will have 11 defensive players on the field at the same time.

OFFENSE

The offense is built to score points and "have the ball" (you'll see and hear this phrase a lot). They do this by either passing or running the ball to move into a better position to score. Players either carry the ball in their possession and move it downfield or they help by blocking for the person carrying the ball. Football teams can score using one or two big plays, or by moving the ball in a more deliberate fashion, methodically marching down the field. A quick scoring offense can help put many points on the scoreboard or successfully come from behind, while a more methodical offense can help run time off the clock and keep the ball away from the other team. A balanced approach is almost always best. The more ways an offense can score, the more difficult it is to defend.

DEFENSE

The defense is a group of players assembled to prevent the other team's offense from scoring. Defenses have plays and strategies of their own designed to react to the offense and attempt to get the ball back in the hands of their own team's offense as soon as possible. Think about the defense as protecting their end zone. On every play, the defensive goal is to stop passing plays by trying to sack the quarterback or prevent a receiver from making a catch, and to limit the success of running plays. Though unproven, there's a saying in football that defense wins championships. A team that cannot score, cannot win.

WHY IS THE FOOTBALL SHAPED LIKE THAT?

The shape of a football is a prolate spheroid (we'll spare you the geometry lesson) and it is a throwback to when a pig's bladder was used to play (you may sometimes hear the football referred to as a "pigskin"). Each football is 11 to 11 ¼ inches long, has a weight of 14 to 15 ounces when inflated, and is made of a urethane "bladder" surrounded by a brown leather covering. On the outside is the NFL commissioner's signature. One distinctive feature of any football is the white laces used to tie the leather together.

All official game footballs are made by the Wilson Sporting Goods Company. Each NFL team provides 12 footballs (and has 12 backups available) to be used during each game they play. The game's referees determine if the footballs given to them meet the required specifications and can be used in the game.

THE NATIONAL FOOTBALL LEAGUE

The NFL is a group of 32 franchises (or teams) that plays professional American football. The **commissioner** oversees the day-to-day operations of the NFL and is the chief executive officer of the NFL. Hired by the franchises' owners, the commissioner enforces the rules established by the league, as well as what is contained in the **collective bargaining agreement** (or **CBA**), between the owners and the **NFL Players Association**.

The league negotiates contracts with sponsors and television networks, with the revenue shared among all the teams. This revenue pays the players' salaries and has been increasing almost every year for decades, with businesses dishing out massive amounts of dollars for the right to be associated with the reach, popularity, and success of the NFL. The league organizes major events like the annual **NFL Draft** (when the teams select incoming players from NCAA college teams) and the final game of the year that determines the champion for the season. The NFL office is also in charge of putting together the annual season schedules, an announcement that makes headlines during the off-season.

Although there may be only 18 weeks to the NFL schedule, with games played for less than half the calendar year, running the biggest and most profitable sports league in North America is a full-time, year-round job. There are ongoing committees of owners and front office personnel discussing ways to improve the game or working on the details of The Big Game or NFL Draft years away.

Even though every NFL season is run much like seasons before, each one brings its own set of issues that must be researched, negotiated, and resolved if possible. That, in short, is the job of the NFL: to prepare for the future by learning from the past, while finding new ways to enhance the game and give the fans what they want, resulting in a growing revenue stream for owners and players. With that growing revenue stream a near certainty, the other valued currencies of success for teams in the NFL are winning games and championships.

CONFERENCES

The NFL's 32 teams are divided into two 16-team groups called conferences: the **American Football Conference (AFC)** and the **National Football Conference (NFC)**. The conferences were established prior to the 1970 season, when the two national professional leagues—the American Football League with 10 teams and the National Football League with 16 teams—merged to create one organization. The original AFC teams mostly came from the American Football League, though some original NFL teams were moved to the AFC to balance out the two conferences at 13 each. The remaining NFL teams made up the NFC. As the NFL expanded, teams were added equally to the AFC and NFC to keep both conferences the same size.

These conferences are important to teams and fans because the NFL creates its annual schedules and bases its playoff system on the standings within each conference. Strong rivalries within each conference have solidified over the years with thrilling plays, stunning upsets, and memorable players. Teams only compete against other teams in their own conference for playoff spots. Conference play also determines how many games are broadcasted. Television networks bid on airing AFC or NFC games, with the winner obtaining the right to broadcast the bulk of their games.

NATIONAL FOOTBALL CONFERENCE

The National Football Conference has four four-team divisions based mostly upon geography:

NFC EAST	NFC NORTH	NFC SOUTH	NFC WEST
Dallas Cowboys	Chicago Bears	Atlanta Falcons	Arizona Cardinals
Philadelphia Eagles	Detroit Lions	Carolina Panthers	Los Angeles Rams
New York Giants	Green Bay Packers	New Orleans Saints	San Francisco 49ers
Washington Commanders	Minnesota Vikings	Tampa Bay Buccaneers	Seattle Seahawks

The easiest way for any team to reach the postseason is to win their division. They do this by having the best record among their four-team group. Every division winner earns at least one home playoff game, which in the NFL has proven to be an advantage in helping teams win. The current playoff format has the team in each conference with the best record earn a **bye**, or week off, in the first round of the playoff while all the other teams play, and home field advantage through the playoffs should they continue to win.

The American Football Conference also has four four-team divisions:

AFC EAST	AFC NORTH	AFC SOUTH	AFC WEST
Buffalo Bills	Baltimore Ravens	Houston Texans	Denver Broncos
Miami Dolphins	Cincinnati Bengals	Indianapolis Colts	Kansas City Chiefs
New England Patriots	Cleveland Browns	Jacksonville Jaguars	Las Vegas Raiders
New York Jets	Pittsburgh Steelers	Tennessee Titans	Los Angeles Chargers

Like the NFC, the four AFC divisional winners all earn playoff spots, and the team with the best record in the conference earns a bye week. The division winners from both conferences are ranked from No. 1 to No. 4 in the playoff seedings (rankings) based upon record; each conference has three additional wild card teams seeded fifth, sixth, and seventh.

The AFC is sometimes called the "junior circuit" because many of its teams came from the old AFL, making them younger than the NFC teams on the "senior circuit." Three original NFL teams—the Cleveland Browns, Indianapolis Colts (originally the Baltimore Colts), and Pittsburgh Steelers—were moved to the AFC to balance out the league when the AFL and NFL merged.

WHY ARE THE AFC WEST TEAMS SO FAR APART?

Because all of the AFL teams remained together to form the AFC after the merger with the National Football League in 1970, the AFC West was made up of teams from three different times zones: the Kansas City Chiefs in the Central time zone, the Denver Broncos in Mountain, and the then-San Diego Chargers and then-Oakland Raiders on Western time. Because these teams had been playing for almost a decade prior to the merger, they already had natural rivalries and breaking them up was deemed a bad idea. As a result, the AFC West begins in the Midwest, goes over the Rocky Mountains, through the desert, and ends at the Pacific Ocean.

FOOTBALL AND TELEVISION

As much as any other sport, the NFL is, shall we say, picture perfect for television. The sounds and the speed of the athletes showing off their skills is something made for high-definition, with many dedicated fans buying new TVs in time for The Big Game. Regular season games are aired for free on network television (CBS, Fox, NBC) in local markets, and viewers can purchase cable or streaming plans in order to watch games not aired in their part of the United States, mostly for out-of-town teams. Outlets like Yahoo Sports and the NFL mobile app allow free streaming on your mobile device of any game broadcast in your television market, including local and primetime games. Both ESPN and Amazon Prime get in on the action as the networks for Monday Night Football and Thursday Night Football, respectively. There are also plans that fans can purchase to listen to a team's home radio broadcasters rather than hearing the calls of a network's play-by-play and color commentators.

Two other football and television milestones were the launch of the NFL Sunday Ticket and the Red Zone Channel. Created by DIRECTV, the Sunday Ticket lets NFL fans watch any football game they want, even when a different game is broadcast in their part of the United States.

FOOTBALL SCHEDULE

All the major broadcast networks currently have rights to some NFL games. CBS and Fox Sports broadcast Sunday games, which begin at 1:00 p.m. Eastern time and continue with a second set of games starting at 4:05 or 4:25 p.m. Eastern. NBC airs Sunday Night Football games, which begin at 8:15 p.m. Eastern. Amazon Prime starts the week off with Thursday Night Football while ABC/ESPN provides football fans the last game of the week during Monday Night Football. The games deemed the most important are often the Sunday Night Football games, since most people are able to watch them and the league has some flexibility to move Sunday games around to maximize viewership and air a compelling matchup. This sometimes means the networks will broadcast games in the other time slots that have little impact on the playoff chase and are only important to a small number of fans.

FOOTBALL SEASON

The NFL season officially begins right after Labor Day and currently lasts 18 weeks, ending during the second week of January. This makes the NFL a three-season sport because it starts in late summer, is played through the fall, and sees the regular season end in winter. As the seasons change, so too do NFL teams. Weather becomes a factor, making it more difficult to use certain offensive plays such as long passes when the cold rain or snow is falling during a game, or the wind chill factor is below zero. As a result, teams will often rely on their defense and an offensive running game later in the season, whereas in the warmer months, they might be more willing to pass the ball. Of course, for fans, attending games in the colder winter months can be a true test of loyalty, even if a team is fighting for a playoff spot.

PRESEASON

All NFL teams conduct a preseason **training camp**, part of which includes each franchise playing at least three games to help prepare for the **regular season**. Camps open in late July or early August, with each team inviting around 80 or 90 players to compete to fill out their 53-player roster. Although many positions are already filled (for example, many players are often under contract and do not have to compete to keep their positions), the extra players are normally free agents or undrafted players who are just looking for a chance to make a team. The extra players are always needed for drills and practices, and because star players don't play much in preseason games. Sometimes one of these players will surprise a team by practicing well or by having a breakout performance during a preseason game, earning a spot on the opening day roster. Most teams allow fans to watch the early preseason practices, giving them a glimpse of what their team might look like to start the season.

REGULAR SEASON

Teams currently play 17 regular season games during an 18-week regular season. Each team faces their three divisional opponents twice, once at their home field and once on the road, for a total of six games. Each team also faces all the teams from another division in their conference on a rotating basis, adding four more games to their schedule. Teams also play the four teams from another division of the conference they are not in, making up four more games on their schedule. They also play the teams that finished in the same place as they did from the two divisions they don't play in their own conference. The 17th game is an inter-conference match, pairing up teams that finish in the same place in their division standings from the prior season.

Let's use the Buffalo Bills 2021 season as an example to help illustrate the building of a team's schedule. The Buffalo Bills are in the AFC East so they were automatically scheduled to play the other AFC East teams—New England Patriots, New York Jets, and Miami Dolphins—twice, for a total of six games. They were scheduled to play their divisional games against the AFC South, so they faced the Tennessee Titans, Indianapolis Colts, Houston Texans, and Jacksonville Jaguars once each, bringing the total to 10 games. The AFC East was scheduled to play its inter-conference games against the NFC South, so the Bills played the Tampa Bay Buccaneers, New Orleans Saints, Carolina Panthers, and Atlanta Falcons, adding four more games for a total of 14 games. Finally, because Buffalo placed first in the AFC East in 2020, it was scheduled to play the remaining two other first-place division teams in the AFC—the Pittsburgh Steelers (AFC North) and Kansas City Chiefs (AFC West)—and the Washington Commanders (winners of the NFC East in 2020), rounding out their schedule of 17 games.

THE PLAYOFFS

The **NFL Playoffs** are the most important games of the year as they determine which teams reach The Big Game. Playoffs begin the weekend after the regular season ends, when six teams from each conference play. A seventh team from each conference, the No. 1 seeds that finished with the best record in each conference, have a bye week, giving them a chance to rest while all the other teams are playing. The other advantage of being the No. 1 seed is that all the team's playoff games are played on their home field, forcing other teams to travel to them and face the hostile crowds of an unfriendly stadium. These advantages are often important because the teams coming off a bye week benefit from the rest and home-field advantage.

-- FOOTBALL FAQ --
WHAT ARE WILD CARD TEAMS?

Each of the two conferences (AFC and NFC) allow three **wild card teams** to make the postseason every year. These are the teams with the three best records in the conference who were unable to win their divisional championship. These wild card berths have made it possible for some good teams to reach the playoffs in years when a team had a record as good or better than one or more winners of another division. Also, because the NFL season is long, some teams can go on a late season surge or collapse, which does not always show in the final standings.

WILD CARD GAMES

The wild card round is the opening round of the NFL Playoffs. Each conference allows three wild card teams to reach the postseason. Under the current format, three of the four divisional winners, who are seeded second, third, and fourth, play the three wild card teams: The wild card team with the best record is the fifth seed and plays the fourth seed; the second best wild card team is the sixth seed and faces the third seed; and the team with the worst record among the three wild card teams is the seventh seed and faces the second seed in each conference.

It may seem counterintuitive, but it can often be challenging for a divisional winner to face a wild card team. Wild card teams often have great confidence from making the postseason and are usually in a stretch where they have won most of their recent games. This combination can sometimes overcome the difference in talent between the two teams, leading to opening round upsets. Sometimes the wild card team is the better team and peaks at season's end after a slow start.

DIVISIONAL ROUND

The NFL's divisional round sees the remaining four teams from each conference play against one another. The top-seeded team from each conference plays after their bye week and hosts the lowest seeded remaining team in the postseason. The other two teams in the conference will also play, with the second-highest remaining seed hosting the game against the third-highest seed. These games normally have many of the NFL's best teams from that season play one another—sometimes against a heated rival or in a rematch from a regular season game, and other times for the first time in years.

The goal is simple in these games—win and advance, because the losers of these games see their promising seasons come to a gut-wrenching end. Head coaches and assistant coaches can be fired for losing divisional round games they should win; players who come up short have to carry that reputation with them and can be traded or released if their team felt they were unable to perform during a pressure-packed playoff game.

CONFERENCE CHAMPIONSHIP GAMES

The two survivors of the intense divisional round playoff games in each conference meet in the conference championship games. This game is often a battle against fatigue as much as it is a competition against the other team. Reaching the conference championship is something many NFL players never have a chance do. This game, it's been said, can sometimes be more difficult than winning The Big Game because the pressure of being this close to the championship can make even the strongest player crack.

That said, these games present plenty of opportunities for players to become legends by helping their franchises reach The Big Game. A year's worth of work rides on these two games every season, and only two of the four teams can move on.

THE BIG GAME

Since 1967, the football season has ended with The Big Game, which pits the winner of the AFC against the winner of the NFC to battle it out for the championship. This game is not only the most important event on the sports calendar, but it's also an entertainment juggernaut, drawing top-notch musicians for its national anthem performance and half-time show, and celebrity spectators from every industry. For decades, The Big Game has been the most watched television show of the year.

For players and coaches, their NFL legacies are written at this game. Bad performances can haunt players for their entire careers and even in retirement, while those who win are celebrated for years as their place in NFL history is etched in stone.

These games are assigned a number to make each game unique, but those numbers are represented in Roman numerals to add some drama. For example, Super Bowl X (10), Super Bowl XXII (22), etc.

WHAT DO THEY WIN?

The winners receive a check from the NFL. The game's **Most Valuable Player** has, in recent years, received a vehicle, and every member of the team is bestowed a game-winning ring. The rings are the most coveted of all the perks because they can be worn for a lifetime, allowing every player to tell the world they were once an NFL champion. There's gamesmanship in designing game rings, as each winning team feels the need to outdo the prior season's champions. These rings can cost tens of thousands of dollars each to make, and are often adorned with gems of the same color as the winning team colors, making for some fascinating designs.

THE VINCE LOMBARDI TROPHY

Named for the coach of the Green Bay Packers, winners of the first two championship games, the Vince Lombardi Trophy is awarded to the winner of The Big Game every season. Each team receives its own unique trophy made of silver with an engraving noting the score, the team they defeated, and the date of the game.

The Lombardi Trophy is normally part of every team's celebration parade and rally when they return to their hometown after The Big Game. It also becomes a centerpiece of every team's display case at their headquarters or practice facility to remind all players to focus on the goal every time they show up for work.

HALFTIME SHOW

As much of a show as the game itself, the halftime show has become a major part of the championship game's activities and has turned the entire experience into an event. Despite not being paid anything, most singers and bands jump at a chance to perform for a record number of viewers, even if it is only for 15 minutes.

Halftime acts are selected by popularity, genre, and performance value (which means you are less likely to see any one-hit wonders make it on stage). It is extremely important for the selected acts to appeal to as many people as possible. However, the NFL is not the one who actually selects the act—they just make up a short list of acts. The honor of choosing the act goes to the host city.

THE PLAYERS

In this chapter, you'll learn about the players you'll see on an NFL field. We'll cover the offense, defense, special teams, and coaches, and describe individual roles and how they fit into the rest of the group. By the end of this chapter, you will have a better understanding of how football players work together as a team.

PLAYERS ON THE FIELD

Though it may look disorganized to a new viewer, most football plays are designed to make use of each player working in conjunction with their teammates. For plays to be successful, each player must know their role during the play, as well as everyone else's.

Each team can have 11 players on the field for a total of 22. If a team has more than 11 players on the field, they can be penalized (see Penalties, page 64).

OFFENSIVE PLAYERS

The responsibility of offensive players, or "the offense," is to make plays that put their team in position to score points and then to score those points. The offense is made up of different types of players, some handling the football while others protect the football and the player carrying the football. As a viewer, if you know a player's position, you'll also know what their role on each play will be, regardless of whether the offense is running or passing the ball. Let's take a look at the different offensive positions on the field, and what the role of each player is within a team's offense. You will soon understand that though a team has only one offense, that group is made up of smaller groups that need to work together for the entire unit to have success.

CENTER

Every offensive play begins with the **center** giving (**snapping**) the football to the quarterback. The center plays in the middle of a five-player unit called the "**offensive line.**" He is normally the captain, or leader, of the offensive line because it is the center's responsibility to tell the other linemen what to do on each play. The job of the center is to make sure the offensive line is blocking the correct defensive players to protect the quarterback during a **pass attempt**, or to block for the running back on a **run attempt**. The center is literally in the middle of all the action, determining blocking assignments for his offensive line on each play.

QUARTERBACK

QB
The main purpose of the **quarterback** is to throw or hand-off the ball to another player so that player can gain yards and score points. Digging a little deeper, the quarterback is tasked with making the most important decisions on the field. Once the ball is in the quarterback's hands, they must try to understand what the defense is doing to stop their offense, and then react within a matter of seconds. They decide who to throw the ball to, who to hand off to, or if they should try to run to gain yards. Although plays are often decided by the coach before the snap, the quarterback may change the play at the line of scrimmage; they will do this if they read the defense and see an opportunity, a **mismatch**, or an issue with the defense's positions and strategy. The quarterback's decisions impact every play and, fair or not, the quarterback performances are the most dissected of any player, and they often take the praise for a win or the blame for a loss.

LEFT AND RIGHT OFFENSIVE GUARDS

G
Playing on each side of the center are **offensive guards**. These players help protect the middle of the offensive line, creating the **pocket**, which is the space behind the line that the quarterback uses to read the defense and throw the ball. Guards are very important to the offensive line because their job is to protect the ball as much as the ball carrier in the first few seconds after the ball is snapped. Guards are often very athletic as well, which allows some offenses to use them as lead blockers on running plays. Depending on the play called, the guards could either focus on blocking to clear a lane at the line of scrimmage for the ball carrier to run through, or could run ahead of the ball carrier and block the first defender they see. As part of the offensive line, guards are an important part of both the running and passing game of every offense and each play called.

LEFT AND RIGHT OFFENSIVE TACKLES

T

Playing next to the offensive guards on either side of the center are the **offensive tackles**. They are the offensive linemen on the edge of the line who protect the quarterback or ball carrier from defensive players trying to go around the offensive line to make a tackle. Offensive tackles are the players most associated with pass blocking for the quarterback. They are normally the strongest of the offensive linemen and block the best defensive linemen from the other team. For a right-handed throwing quarterback who faces right when throwing and can't see who is behind them, the left offensive tackle protects the quarterback's blind side on passing plays, thus putting the most pressure on that position to give the quarterback time. Like offensive guards, tackles also block on running plays to clear a lane for the ball carrier at the line of scrimmage, or block a defender further downfield. This position is one of the most physically demanding on a football field.

TIGHT ENDS

TE

Lining up next to an offensive tackle on many plays are **tight ends**, who are used to block or catch passes during a game. Teams may employ one, two, or even three tight ends during a play, and have them do a multitude of things on the field. Tight ends are not normally fast, but they are bigger and stronger than most other players, which is why they are sometimes used to block. That is also why tight ends catch passes over the middle of the field, as a hard hit from a defensive player often won't faze them. A great tight end can turn those caught passes into touchdowns, which is why their role is so important. The skill set of a tight end opens the possibility of a wide range of play-calling options, which keeps the defense guessing during a game. Think of a tight end as the Swiss Army knife of an offense.

RUNNING BACKS

RB While tight ends start plays next to linemen, **running backs** are often positioned in the **backfield** behind or next to the quarterback. As their name suggests, the job of the running back is to carry the ball and gain yards on every play. There are generally two types of running backs: shifty and fast, or strong and bruising. Offensive plays are normally designed to have a running back go one way or the other when carrying the ball; however, if there is a missed block, a talented running back can either bulldoze over the defenders or quickly pivot in the opposite direction where there are often fewer defensive players. Running backs can also be used in the passing game, but if they can't catch—and some can't—that will not be part of the coach's game plan. They also may be called upon to stay in the pocket and block a defender that is going after the quarterback. With the right skills, a running back can be very valuable to any offensive team.

The most common types of running backs are **halfbacks**, **wingbacks**, and **fullbacks**. Halfbacks are the type of running back that usually lines up behind the quarterback and runs the ball when a run play is called. Wingbacks are the more versatile type of running back, that can either run or catch passes. Lastly, you have fullbacks that perform more blocking than running. Fullbacks are generally bigger and stronger than the other types of running backs, and on most occasions they provide blocking for another running back within the same play.

WIDE RECEIVERS

WR One of the most important members of any quarterback's passing game are the **wide receivers**; their primary goal is to catch passes and gain as many yards as they can after making the catch. They're usually the fastest and tallest players on the field and can outrun almost anyone, including those on the defense. Though most times wide receivers are tackled right after making the catch, they can often take a short pass and turn it into a big gain by running with the ball after the catch; or, if everything aligns, the quarterback will send a long pass sailing down the field for the wide receiver to catch, possibly even into the end zone. Some wide receivers may be asked to block for running backs. In the NFL today, having more than one above-average wide receiver makes an offense difficult to defend.

DEFENSIVE PLAYERS

The defense is on the field to stop the opposing offense from advancing the ball and scoring points. Since it is normally easier to act than to react in a physical contest, on a football field, defense is usually considered tougher to play than offense. You need bigger, stronger, and faster players on defense to overcome the fact that offensive players know where they are going while defenders can only react to what they see happening. This section of the chapter explains the primary roles of each defensive player on the field and how together they can execute and succeed in keeping the offense out of **scoring position**.

DEFENSIVE TACKLES

DT
X

Defensive tackles line up closest to the football when a play begins and, along with the defensive ends, make up the defensive linemen. A defensive tackle's primary goal is to stop the ball carrier from going up the middle of the field. Defensive linemen often line up in different positions from one play to the next; this allows a defensive lineman to line up against a specific offensive lineman, one that they don't believe can pass or run block them. This movement may also be designed to create a hole, or large gap, in the offensive line, allowing another defensive player to run through and make the tackle.

If a defensive tackle is very good, the offense may try to double team him by having two people block that player in the hopes of slowing him down. This position is one that most people only notice when they've tackled a runner deep in the backfield, made a mistake missing a tackle, or allowed a large gap for the runner to go through. The success of defensive tackles makes possible everything else a defense wants to do.

DEFENSIVE ENDS

DE
X

Defensive ends are the "glamour" position of the line because they are the players that often create big plays by sacking the quarterback and creating fumbles to help their team get the ball. Defensive ends try to get past the offensive blockers using quickness to sprint around or outrun them so they can either tackle the player carrying the ball or sack the quarterback. It is important for defensive ends to do well against running plays because if the defense can't stop it, an offense will continue to run the ball at them, grinding out yardage on each play as they march down the field while the clock continues to wind down. This can lead to a tired defense being on the field for a long time and, since there will be fewer passes, also limits the opportunities for a defensive end to **rush** and sack the quarterback during a game, which they *love* to do.

LINEBACKERS

LB
X

Playing behind the defensive line are a group called **linebackers**. Normally, linebackers play in groups of three or four, with each assigned an area to patrol and make tackles when called upon. On passing plays, often some of the linebackers will work with defensive linemen to run toward the quarterback at the same time from the same direction, making it difficult for the offensive linemen to block everyone; other linebackers stay in their assigned area to guard wide receivers or tight ends passing through, or even run along with the wide receiver or tight end to defend against a **pass completion**. The "front seven," as they are often called, work together on both running and passing plays, with the defensive lineman engaging the offense first, and the linebackers coming up from behind to make tackles. So, while linemen and linebackers might be on different units of the defense, their teamwork on the field is important for any NFL team's success.

CORNERBACKS

CB
X

Cornerbacks are part of the passing defense of every foot-ball team. They are often called upon to guard one wide receiver during a play and can be asked to guard the same wide receiver for an entire game. Some football teams play a **zone defense**, which is when a cornerback protects a portion of the field and is expected to stop any receiver who enters his zone. While defensive ends make highlights from sacking the quarterback, cor-nerbacks become popular by intercepting passes, giving their team possession of the football at the spot where they are tackled with the ball. Some cornerbacks are fast enough to avoid tackles and reach the end zone after the interception, thus scoring a touchdown for their team. Cornerbacks can also help defend running plays by the offense, but they are rarely close enough to the ball to make tackles unless the runner has broken free with a longer gain down the field.

SAFETIES

S
X

Safeties are the last line of defense on a football field. They play far away from the line of scrimmage, normally 20 to 30 yards downfield or close to the end zone when needed. They are there to tackle a runner or wide receiver carrying the ball that far down the field or to provide help to the cornerbacks defending against a pass. Each defense usually has two safeties, with each normally covering half the width of the football field. Later in the game, some teams will add a third safety to help cover the field better. During running plays, if a defense is having a hard time stopping the offense, sometimes one of the safeties will play closer to the line of scrimmage to try and make a tackle. They are also used to rush toward the quarterback for a sack on passing plays, through **blitzing** (see page 111), if a defense needs a big play.

SPECIAL TEAMS

Every NFL team has a special teams unit, a group of players who work together on a select set of kicking plays. Football teams will kick the ball when they are starting the game or the second half, when they are trying to score a field goal or extra point, or when they are giving possession of the ball back to the opposition. There are two specific kinds of kicker, and a unique group of players are on the field for the play. In this portion of the chapter, we will point out a few of the important positions on the special teams, what their roles are, and what makes them so important to their teams. After this section you will understand what makes special teams so special.

PUNTER

P

A football team's **punter** is called upon when the offense comes up short on reaching the first down marker before getting into field goal range or scoring a touchdown, and they need to give the ball back to the opposition. Sometimes it is more important for receiving teams to gain yards after catching the punt, but other times their goal may be to block the punt. During those times, it is very important for the punter not to let their kick get blocked. If it is blocked, the receiving team can recover the ball and run it toward their end zone. When successful, most punters can kick the ball more than half the length of the football field and high in the air with enough hang time to allow their team time to get down-field to defend the return. They can also place it where no one will be able to catch it, often resulting in the ball rolling farther down the field, leaving the opposition with worse field position farther away from their end zone.

KICK RETURNER

KR A football team's **kick returner** is the person responsible for catching the football after a kickoff and advancing the ball toward the end zone until tackled. An effective kick returner is one that is either fast and/or shifty to gain positive yards on every kickoff return. The importance of a good kick returner cannot be overstated, because they provide the starting point for an offense's upcoming drive.

GUNNER

When a team is giving up possession by punting, the **gunner** is called to the field as part of the special teams unit. The gunner's job is to make it down the field while the punt is in the air and to be ready to make a tackle to limit the number of yards the other team's player can run after a catch. If the kick is in the air long enough, or if the gunner is fast enough, he may reach the ball before the person catching it, forcing the kick returner to fair catch the punt. A fair catch is when a kick returner puts his arm up in the air, telling the other team they won't run as long as they're allowed to make the catch without being hit.

PLACEKICKER

K A **placekicker** is the person a football team will turn to for the kickoff to start a game or the second half, and when they need to kick a field goal. No matter the distance of the field goal kick, the placekicker will line up about seven yards behind the line of scrimmage to allow enough room to kick the ball without it being blocked. Longer kicks are hit with a lower arc, making them easier to block, while shorter kicks are often still rising when they hit the **net** behind the **goal posts**. For kickoffs, the objective is usually to kick the ball into the end zone so that there is no risk of a big return play by the other team. When this happens, the ball is placed at the 25 yard line and the receiving team's offense begins there. Place-kickers always need to consider the direction of the wind as they line up for the kick, while also making sure their footing is strong enough to prevent them from slipping as they strike the football.

HOLDER

Placekick **holders** are the people who receive the snap and hold the ball in place during a field goal attempt. You will also see them trying to rotate the ball to have the white laces on the football face away from the placekicker. This is to ensure the football flies straighter after it is hit while also making it less painful for the kicker to hit the ball with his foot. A holder will often see the kicker put a hole in the ground with his finger; the holder's goal is to put the nose of the football in that hole because that is where the kicker will be aiming. A holder is not required for kickoffs, unless it is unusually windy or there are poor weather conditions; otherwise, the ball usually sits on a tee.

LONG SNAPPER

The **long snapper** is the lineman that snaps the ball to the holder on a field goal attempt or directly to the punter for a punt. While the distance is always the same between the long snapper and the holder or punter, the long snapper is only able to see the holder or punter upside down by looking between his legs. As a result, these players spend a lot of time together on the practice field working on just the right height and speed of a long snap in order to make both the holder and the placekicker or the punter happy. If successful with their timing, a placekicker will normally end up getting points for their team and a punter will have an opportunity to better execute a successful punt in terms of distance and placement.

HOW CAN PLAYERS KEEP GETTING HIT AND THEN GET RIGHT BACK UP?

Football is a high-speed, high-contact sport with at least one person hitting the ground hard and several players hitting each other hard on every play. As a result, every player on the field wears many pieces of equipment to help keep them injury-free. Starting at the top, every player wears a helmet. Although decorated in the team's colors and often with the team's logo, helmets are much more than a fashion statement. They are designed to prevent concussions, which are a very serious head injury. Helmets also come with face guards to prevent objects from flying into a player's face during play. Face shields are often added for further protection of players' eyes. Another smaller yet important piece of safety equipment is a mouth guard, which is worn to protect the players' teeth, tongue, lips, and jaw.

Every player wears shoulder pads to protect their upper bodies. The pads are worn underneath a players' jersey, so they are not exposed at any time during a game. Pads protect both the front and back of a players' chest and shoulders when they are either being hit or when they are hitting/ tackling someone. Smaller pads are always worn to protect a player's hips, knees, and thighs because, in the NFL, a player's legs draw as much contact from other players and the ground as their chest. These pads are sewn into a player's uniform and are mandatory in today's game, whereas in the past they were voluntary.

COACHES

Putting together a good coaching staff is important for a successful NFL team. There are many paths to becoming one of the multiple coaches on an NFL coaching staff, including starting out as a player or moving over from a college coaching role. Some players join the coaching ranks when their NFL playing career is over; others do not have the talent to play beyond high school or college, but choose to stay in the game by becoming coaches. Those with little NFL or coaching experience may land entry level coaching jobs with an NFL team, usually starting out by reviewing footage of their team's next opponent or helping the head coach run practice effectively and efficiently. Each coach's path is the journey through the ranks, with some rising all the way to the top as the head coach of a team.

HEAD COACH

An NFL **head coach** is akin to a company's chief operating officer. They oversee the team's most valuable assets, the players, and put them in the best position to win games during the season. Head coaches define the team culture and the approach to their practices and games. They are usually very involved in the offensive and defensive game plan each week. They are year-round teachers of playing football, working during the offseason, training camp, and during the regular season.

OFFENSIVE COORDINATOR

An **offensive coordinator** works with a team's offensive players to come up with a game plan for each opponent. The offensive coordinator will study every opponent's defense, find their weaknesses, and try to exploit them. Working with the head coach, the offensive coordinator finds the best plays from their **playbook**, and to maximize their effectiveness, they practice the plays that best suit the defense they will be facing. Offensive coordinators also determine the players assigned to be on the field for every play.

DEFENSIVE COORDINATOR

The **defensive coordinator** is the coach matched up against the opponent's offensive coordinator. They are coaching directly against each other in their play calling and game plan. The defensive coordinator needs to understand what an offensive team is trying to do during a play and stop it. They study the upcoming opponent's offense to identify tendencies in play calling or clues to what the offense might do. The defensive coordinator will try to surprise the opposition with different types of plays during the game to stop the offense; they do their best to limit the number of points the opposing offense can score.

SPECIAL TEAMS COACH

The **special teams coach** helps a football team find success in the kicking game. They create a **blocking scheme** to allow their team to advance the ball when receiving kicks or when kicking field goals. They also lead the team's strategy on kickoffs regarding where to place the ball or how to get downfield to tackle as quickly as possible. Being a special teams coach is difficult because the players, such as gunners and blockers, often change, making it tough for them to develop a rhythm.

QUARTERBACK COACH

Many NFL teams will employ a coach to work solely with their quarterback. Often a former quarterback or offensive coordinator, the **quarterback coach** will help the quarterback look at game footage to understand what a defense will try to do against them. They are on the sidelines during the game and will discuss with the quarterback how the defense reacted to certain plays; together, they adjust what the quarterback does the next time to increase the chances of success. They also help correct or improve throwing and handoff techniques.

GENERAL MANAGERS

General managers, often referred to as GMs, work with the head coach to find the best players who fit into the team's methods of playing offense and defense. They have a team of **scouts** who look for players in college before the draft and check out other teams' players in case they want to make a trade. Being a GM also requires a good understanding of the **salary cap**, because there are limits to the amount of money they can spend on players each season. The GM may also be the person who hires the head coach, and their working relationship can get tricky if they don't get along or don't have winning seasons. The success of the team is often shared by the head coach and general manager, and if a team fails for too many seasons in a row, both are often fired at the same time.

Fantasy Football

Fantasy football, a sport of its own these days, is where fans become armchair GMs selecting and developing their own team and competing week to week with others within their league. Real-life NFL players are "drafted" onto a fantasy player's team, and that team is matched up against another fantasy player's team each week of the NFL season. The goal is for the players on your team to score more fantasy football points than your opponent's players.

Here's how it works: When the real-life NFL players make a play on the field, the fantasy players are given a pre-determined number of points. For example: Your fantasy league has determined that touchdowns are worth 6 points, 20 pass yards are worth 1 point, and 10 receiving yards are worth 1 point. Quarterback 1 and Receiver 2 are both on the same team in real life, but Quarterback 1 is your quarterback and Receiver 2 is on your fantasy opponent's team. During the real game, Quarterback 1 throws a 20-yard pass to Receiver 2 for a touchdown. In this scenario, your fantasy team would gain 7 points (6 for the touchdown and 1 for the 20 pass yards thrown) and your opponent's fantasy team would gain 8 points (6 for the touchdown and 2 for the 20 receiving yards).

To make things more manageable, defenses and special teams are often drafted as a group when playing fantasy football. That means if a kick returner scores a touchdown, the fantasy teams who drafted that real-life team's defense and special teams are credited with a score. The same holds true for when a defense intercepts a quarterback during a game, because they earn points for a turnover in fantasy football leagues. If that interception is turned into a touchdown, fantasy owners earn points for both. Note that points are detracted for missed plays, so in the case of an interception, the quarterback who threw it will be docked points.

Continued >>

Many fantasy leagues are designed where NFL players are drafted for an entire season, although players can usually be dropped and available players added on a weekly basis up until a certain date or even throughout the season. These fantasy players see their team matched up against another team from their league on a week-to-week basis, with the high score winning. These leagues, which are often just groups of friends and family who love watching football, sometimes hold draft parties to select their teams and can even offer prizes to the league winner. This kind of draft can often be prepared for over weeks, with sports media outlets offering guides and opinions to finding the best players at every position.

There are also daily fantasy sports that fans can enjoy, where they pick different players from week to week. In this game, fantasy GMs select players at every position while staying under a salary cap. They are then matched up against a group of other teams, and the player scoring the most points wins. This type of fantasy is usually played through a national league, such as DraftKings or FanDuel.

OFFICIALS

Game **officials** on the field make sure the NFL rules are followed and call penalties by throwing a small yellow **flag** on the field when they occur during play. Officials work their way up the ranks, beginning at the high school or college level before becoming NFL officials. There are seven officials on the field for pro football games, led by the **referee** who makes the announcements of the penalties. Next is the **umpire**, the official who handles the football between plays and marks off penalty yardage. Along the line of scrimmage are the **down judge** and the **line judge**, who make sure players don't jump **offsides** before the snap. Down the field (20 to 25 yards from the line of scrimmage) are the **field judge** and **side judge**. They are the officials who call pass interference penalties and decide if receivers were in or out of bounds when making sideline catches. The **back judge** lines up in the middle of the field about 30 yards away from the football and calls pass interference penalties while also overseeing when the television networks take a commercial break. In chapter 3, we will explain in more detail the various types of penalties and what happens after an incorrect or controversial call. Officials have a huge impact on the game and can thus be reasonably (or unreasonably) blamed or credited for the outcome.

-- FOOTBALL FAQ --
HOW DO THEY DECIDE WHO WEARS WHAT UNIFORM?

Every NFL team has its own unique game day uniform. Most NFL teams have a uniform that incorporates a white jersey with colored names and numbers. Teams also have a uniform, sometimes multiple uniforms, using their franchise's official team color as the primary color with other colors to provide accents and for names and numbers. The home team for every NFL game chooses which uniform they are going to wear for that game in advance, while the visiting team wears the opposite jersey. (So if a home team chooses to wear their white jerseys, the visiting team will have to wear their team colors, and vice versa.) This makes it easier for game officials as well as the fans to know which player is with which team. Sometimes you will see both teams in their team official colored jerseys; but that only comes with league approval if it has been determined the colors are different enough not to cause any confusion during the game.

THE RULES AND FLOW OF THE GAME

In this chapter, you'll learn how a typical football game unfolds, from what takes place during pre-game to the outcome. We will cover what you, as a new fan, will see take place, and explore the important decisions every team makes that are part of their game strategy.

GAME TIME

From start to finish, most football games last about three hours. That may not make much sense to you, since you already know that there are four 15-minute quarters. So where do the extra two hours come from? This section explores the game while the **play clock** is running, the many reasons the clock stops, and why some quarters last longer than others.

COIN TOSS AND THE START OF THE GAME

Despite all the world's modern technology, a football game still begins as it did a century ago, with a coin flip to determine who gets possession of the football first. The visiting team is given the right to call the coin flip, which they do before the game's referee tosses the coin into the air. The team that wins the coin flip has a choice to make: They may either receive the ball first to start the game, or they can defer and accept possession of the ball to start the second half (third quarter). Some head coaches like to put their offense out onto the field first to try to set the pace of the game, score first, and establish momentum. Other head coaches like knowing that they will have possession after halftime, and they will defer if they win the toss.

The team that loses the coin toss always gets to choose which end zone they would like to defend to start the game. This is important during outdoor games when the wind might be a factor; teams always want the wind behind them to help the passing and kicking game (no one wants to throw or kick against the wind); and, as we discuss later in this chapter, the direction teams run their offense in the first quarter is the same as it will be in the fourth quarter.

KICKOFF

With the opening possession decided, the special teams players for each team line up for the **kickoff**. The ball is placed on a tee at the kicking team's 35-yard line, and the kicker kicks the ball down the field to the opposite team where, ideally, the receiver catches the ball and runs it back up the field for a gain of yards or, in one of the most exciting football plays possible, returns it for a touchdown. If the receiving team feels that there is no opportunity to run the ball back because of the kicking team's defense, the punt returner can wave his arms to signal a fair catch so he doesn't get tackled. The offense then begins possession where the punt returner caught the ball.

Often, the kicker kicks the ball beyond the field of play, either in the end zone or beyond the end zone, without it being touched by any player. This results in a **touchback**: the ball automatically gets placed at the 25-yard line of the receiving team's side of the field, or **terri-tory**. If the ball hits the ground in the field of play, the receiving team can pick it up, making it a **live ball**, and can run to try to advance; or the kicking team can surround the ball and let it bounce farther down the field before touching it to make it a **dead ball**, making that the spot where the offense starts their drive. If the ball touches or glances off any player on the receiving team without being fully caught or controlled, it becomes a live ball that either team can recover. As we mentioned previously, while uncommon, you may see the kicker kick the football out of bounds on either side of the field. If that happens, the receiving team chooses between getting the ball where it went out of bounds, or at the 40 yard line in their territory.

FIRST QUARTER

When the kickoff takes place, the game has *almost* begun. "Almost" because the game clock won't start counting down until a team begins to advance the football. So, if you see the opening kickoff ruled a touchback, the game clock will still read 15:00 when the offense and defense take the field; it won't start running until the offense snaps the ball for the first time. A note on the clock: The clock will continue to run during play and after any play, running or passing, that ends in-bounds. However, the clock will stop if a pass is thrown and falls **incomplete** (including a **spike**), or if the ball carrier goes out of bounds. On an out-of-bounds stoppage, the clock will start again once the official has **spotted** the ball (placed it where the ball was downed).

That probably seems like a lot to remember, but trust me, you will get the hang of it.

Now, unlike some other quarters, if a ball carrier goes out of bounds with possession of the football, the clock will not stop except for the time it takes for the official to get the ball in his hands and return it to the middle of the field to spot the ball. The first quarter is often played rather quickly, because other than the normal timeouts for scoring or change of possession, teams are not in as much of a rush to get off a high number of plays and are more willing to let the game clock run without a reason to intentionally stop it.

SECOND QUARTER

The second quarter begins with each team changing end zones. This means that the direction a team's offense was facing to score in the first quarter will be the opposite of the direction they are facing in the second quarter. This switch tries to make sure one team does not have any weather-related or field-related advantages for the entire game.

Also, while most of the second quarter is played much like the first quarter, there are a few differences. Most notable is the two-minute warning, which is an official timeout when there are two minutes left in the quarter. This rule allows teams to plan a strategy for the remainder of the first half (those final two minutes before halftime can be crucial to the second-half strategy and the eventual outcome of the game). Teams plan a set of plays, called the two-minute offense, to try to dictate the pace and manage the clock after the two-minute warning. Remember that the game clock will stop when a player goes out of bounds with the football, helping an offense that is trying to score more points before halftime.

At the two-minute warning, head coaches are no longer allowed to challenge plays on the field (we'll talk about challenges in more detail later in the chapter); that responsibility goes to the officials in the replay booth watching the game.

THIRD QUARTER

The third quarter begins with the teams going in the same direction as they did in the second quarter, and the team that didn't start the game with possession of the football has it now. Each team has come up with new strategies during halftime, so the first possession in the third quarter is often when some form of scoring takes place. For teams that are behind at halftime, making a comeback begins with doing well early in the third quarter to build momentum, while teams in the lead are looking ahead to make sure that doesn't happen. In a close game, the third quarter may become a reset button, with each team running their best plays.

FOURTH QUARTER

Welcome to the final 15 minutes of the game. The start of the fourth quarter sees teams changing end zones once again, returning them to the directions they were going at the start of the game. This quarter is when clock management becomes a part of the strategy for both teams.

For the team ahead in the game, taking time off the clock is just as important as trying to score more points. The leading team, however, cannot be too conservative in their play calling because keeping possession of the ball and refreshing downs helps them run out the clock, while punting it away gives the other team a chance to catch up and take the lead. This is when a good running game can help an offense because they can advance the ball and get first downs without having to throw often and risk an incompletion; this keeps the clock moving.

For the team behind, making a play on defense, such as a turnover or forcing a punt, is important to get the ball back and try to catch up. These teams will often play more aggressively, hoping to make a big play.

The game clock rules that take effect at the two-minute warning of the second quarter also take effect at the five-minute remaining mark of the fourth quarter. As a reminder, that means any ball carrier that goes out of bounds will stop the clock until it is snapped for the next play. Teams sometimes need to use their timeouts on defense to stop the clock and save time for their offense, in the hopes of getting the ball back with enough time remaining to win the game.

OVERTIME

Everyone loves extra of anything, right? If an NFL game is tied when 60 minutes of play have concluded, the game will go to overtime. There will be a new coin toss to see who receives the ball first, each team gets two timeouts, and all plays are reviewed by game officials. The current overtime rules call for no more than 10 minutes of game play, with each team guaranteed at least one possession unless the team with the ball first scores a touchdown. If that happens, the game ends. If the team with the ball first does not score or scores a field goal, the other team will get a possession, and for each case there are a few game-ending scenarios.

Regardless of the result of the first team's possession (unless it is a touchdown), if the second team with possession in overtime scores a touchdown, they win. Game over. If the team with the ball first did not score, any score wins, meaning a touchdown or field goal wins it for the team with the ball second. If neither scores on their first possession, play continues in sudden-death style where the next score wins. If the team with the ball first scored a field goal, and the second team scores a field goal on their first possession to tie it again, play continues in sudden-death style where the next score wins; but if the second team does not score at all on that first possession, the game is over and they lose.

If neither team scores at all or if they both kick one field goal without scoring again, then the game is declared a tie and goes into the standings as such (though everyone hates ties). Postseason games cannot end in a tie, so the teams would continue playing until the tie is broken to determine a winner.

TIMEOUTS

During regular season games, each NFL team receives three timeouts per half; any unused timeouts from the first half are lost and do not carry over into the second half.

Timeouts are used to stop the clock or to prevent something from going wrong, such as a penalty or a bad play on the field. If a coach or player sees a mismatch or an unexpected lineup from the other team, they may take a timeout to reevaluate the players on the field or change the play call. A "chilling" use of a timeout is to call it just seconds before a placekicker kicks a field goal. This is called **"icing"** the kicker and is meant to let the kicker sit longer with his nerves in hopes of causing a mistake and bad kick.

Timeouts are also used as collateral when challenging plays (we'll talk more about this later in the chapter). If the challenge is successful, the team keeps their time out. However, if their challenge is unsuccessful, they give up one of their timeouts for that half. In the second half, teams are more careful with their timeouts than in the first half in case they need them as part of a comeback late in the game.

BASIC RULES

Here we describe some of the basic rules and occurrences you will see during a game. You'll hear broadcasters use these terms repeatedly, and they will quickly become familiar to you.

Snap of the football: Every play begins with a snap of the football to the quarterback. The "snap," which you may have heard referred to as a **hike**, is simply the exchange of the football from the center to the quarterback, and takes place in one of two ways. If the quarterback is directly behind the center, the ball will be handed to the quarterback, who places both hands between the center's legs. The second type of snap is called a shotgun snap: In this situation, the quarterback will stand roughly five yards behind the center, and will keep his throwing hand on top and his off hand on the bottom as he forms a V. The center will turn the laces of the football upward, snap the ball to the quarterback by tossing it backward through his legs, and the ball should land in the quarterback's throwing hand in a position to make a quick throw.

The play clock, which is the timer used to indicate how long the offense has to snap the ball for each play, is set to either 25 or 40 seconds, depending on the game situation. For example, the play clock is set to 25 seconds after certain administrative stoppages (such as timeout, penalty enforcement, change of possession, etc.), while the play clock will be set to 40 seconds during normal game play immediately after each play ends. If the snap does not occur within that time frame, a penalty is called on the offense and the play clock is reset to start over again. We'll talk more about that later in the chapter.

Down by contact: At the speed pro football is played, sometimes a player is moving so fast that those on the field don't realize that the player with the ball is "down by contact." Any offensive player is deemed to be down if, as a result of contact with a defensive player, any part of his body other than his feet, hands, or wrists makes contact with the ground, which results in the end of the play. This contact can be a passing touch of a defensive player who otherwise missed the tackle, and can even come yards before the ball carrier loses his balance and falls to the ground. The important factor here is that the contact resulted in the eventual fall to the ground. The new line of scrimmage becomes wherever the ball is when the ball carrier is "down" on the ground.

There are some situations in which a player is "down" without a defender's touch. One example is a quarterback going down on one knee upon receiving the snap. This is usually seen at the end of the half or at the end of the game to wind down the clock. Another example we talked about earlier is a kick returner signaling for a fair catch. The returner is considered down upon catching the ball.

Quarterback sack: Many defensive linemen specialize in sacking the quarterback. A sack is when the quarterback is tackled for a

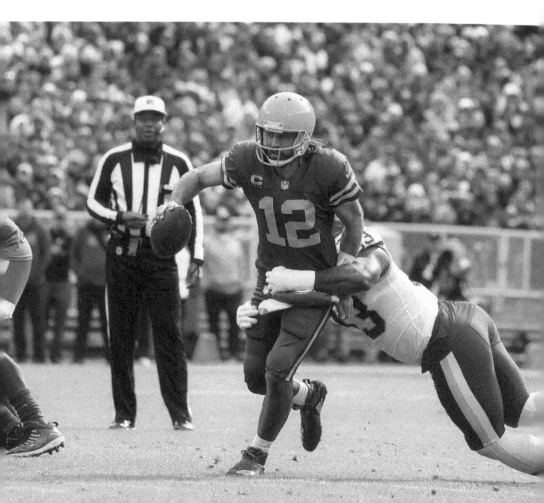

loss of yardage, meaning someone tackled the quarterback behind the original line of scrimmage. This play can make it difficult for the offense to gain a first down, may push them out of **field goal range** (meaning they are too far away from the goal post to kick a field goal), and may give the defense better field position (meaning they are closer to their end zone) when they get the ball back and start on offense. Getting to the quarterback impacts not only that play but also can cause rushed throws, changes in the offensive play-calling strategy, and can intimidate the quarterback if he is fearing a sack at any moment. It also puts the quarterback at a higher risk of injury.

Run-pass option: In recent years the NFL has seen a return of the run-pass option offensive scheme to the game. When using a **run-pass option** (or **RPO**), the quarterback works with a running back in the backfield. After the snap, the quarterback will read how the defense is attacking the play and will react accordingly. If the defense is going after the running back, the quarterback will fake handing the ball to that player and keep it, running in the opposite direction as the running back. The quarterback will then also have an option to pass the ball to a receiver down the field as long as they do not run beyond the line of scrimmage before throwing (which applies to every pass thrown in a game). Although the run-pass option is a risky play to run too often because the quarterback is exposed to more tackles, hits, and potential injuries, it's a good way for some teams to use the athletic ability of their quarterbacks and minimize the number of times they need to throw the ball during a game.

Catch vs. incomplete pass: One of the most often discussed topics during an NFL game is whether a player made a catch or not. In simple terms, a **catch** is when a receiver gains possession of a thrown ball, keeps both feet in bounds, and never lets the football touch the ground. Though it might seem very cut-and-dried, things can get complicated. For example, a wide receiver can't allow the ground to help them maintain possession of the football during a catch, nor can they allow the ground to shake the ball out of their possession before the catch is made (you'll hear the announcers say "the ground can't cause a fumble" with some regularity). In both cases, that becomes an **incomplete pass**. The football can be held against a player's body, including their helmet or even between their legs, and still be considered a catch. It can even roll on the body of a defensive player on the ground before being picked up by an offensive player. If it doesn't touch the ground, it is a catch.

An incomplete pass can sometimes be just as difficult to determine as a catch itself. An incomplete pass happens when a receiver doesn't have or maintain possession of the football, or if they fail to establish both feet in bounds before falling or running out of bounds. An incomplete pass is also called if a defensive player makes contact with the receiver after the receiver touches the ball but is unable to gain possession of the football. This type of play can be mistakenly called a fumble on the field before the **replay officials** determine whether a receiver ever had possession of the pass before it was recovered by the defense for a turnover.

DOWNS, DISTANCE, YARDS, AND HOW IT SHAKES OUT

Here we quickly explain the simple terms of downs and distance, how an offense "gains" a first down, and what they are thinking about when deciding if they need to "go for it" on fourth down or kick the ball away to the other team.

Downs: On each possession, an offense needs to gain at least 10 yards to keep possession of the football. Teams are granted four downs, or chances, to obtain the 10 yards. If successful, the set of four downs renews. On fourth down, however, if they don't get enough yards for the first down, the other team takes possession of the football where the last play ended. If an offense is too close to their own end zone and a failed fourth down play would make it easier for the other team to score when they take possession, instead of attempting to get the yards they need for a new set of downs, they use their fourth down to punt the ball away. If an offense is close enough to score a field goal on fourth down, they will likely kick it to

try to score rather than punt to the other team; this is called "going for it." We only see teams go for it on fourth down a few times each game, sometimes not at all. They tend to make this decision in short yardage situations, meaning only a yard or even inches to gain, or if they are losing late in the game.

Distance: The yard line an offense needs to reach to gain a new set of downs is always 10 yards from the place where they start the current set of downs. If the offense receives a penalty, the team will be pushed back, so they may need to gain more than 10 yards to get that first down. You'll often hear commentators say phrases like "first and ten" or "second and three." This refers to the down the team is on (first or second, in our example) and the number of yards they need to gain before they get a new set of downs (ten and three, respectively). On occasion, you'll hear "third and long" or "fourth and long," noting that the team is short on one of their last tries and has to gain more than five yards to get the new set of downs.

The only time an offense will need to gain less than 10 yards is if they earn a first down inside the defense's 10-yard line, or within 10 yards of the end zone and nearing a score. Then the offense needs to score a touchdown within four plays or has the option of kicking a field goal before the possession ends.

Turnovers: There are two ways a defense can take over possession of the ball from the offense. When a quarterback throws a pass (obviously intended for his own player) and the ball is caught by a defensive player, that is called an interception. The defender who makes the interception is allowed to advance the ball toward his end zone while trying to avoid being tackled. If that player makes it all the way to the end zone for a touchdown, it is called a **pick-six**. This is one of the ways the offense can commit a turnover, which is giving up possession of the football without meaning to or needing to.

Any ball carrier is allowed to advance the football until they either go out of bounds or are tackled by a member of the other team. If, however, they lose possession of the football before either of these things happen, it is called a fumble. A fumble can be picked up by a member of either team and, in most circumstances, can be advanced all the way to his end zone by the recovering player unless tackled or having run out of bounds. Fumbles are another form of turnover and are recorded as such when a team loses possession.

Punt: A punt normally takes place on a team's fourth down when they have failed on the first three downs to gain the required 10 yards and are not within field goal range. The offensive team will send out their punter, who lines up about 15 yards behind the player, called the long snapper, giving them the ball. The defensive team will often try to block the punt in the hopes of preventing it from flying down the field. If that happens, the defense will have created a much shorter field for their offense to score, or may even be able to recover the punt themselves, advance it, and score a touchdown. Most of the time a punt is successful, and the receiving team has a player far downfield who catches the punt and either tries to advance the ball in the direction of their end zone, or calls for a fair catch.

Team 1   0   0· Team 2

1ST 14:19   :14   2ND & 3

-- FOOTBALL FAQ --
WHAT IS ALL THE STUFF ON A SCOREBOARD?

Whether you're at a game or watching on TV, the scoreboard provides important information you need to follow along. First, it gives you the names of the two teams playing—their nickname (or an abbreviation of it), not their hometown name. The visiting team will normally appear on the left, and the home team on the right. The teams' colors are often used as well, so you can easily differentiate between the two.

Next is the current game score, which will appear next to each team's name, as well as a small indicator (often a small shape) of which team currently has possession of the ball (offense). There will also be a game clock showing how much time is left in the quarter, as well as a play clock telling you how much time the team currently on offense has to begin the next play. Near that you will see the down and distance (for example, 2nd and 3) the offense needs to gain to get a first down.

METHODS OF SCORING

There are five ways for a football team to score points, and though one of them can only be achieved by the defense, all of them are available to both teams during every game under the right circumstances. Here we describe each way a team can score, how many points each type of play is worth, and how they all can play into the strategy of a game.

Touchdown: A touchdown is worth six points and is the most points a football team can score at one time. A touchdown is scored when a ball carrier reaches the end zone where their team needs to score. A player cannot score a touchdown in their own end zone (the one their team is defending), only in the end zone their offense is trying to reach. An offensive, defensive, or special teams' player can score a touchdown during an NFL game.

Extra point: An extra point (or point after touchdown) is one option for a team that just scored a touchdown. The kick takes place with the ball around the 23-yard line, making the attempt a 33-yard kick. The placekicker aims the ball through the goal posts (often called the **uprights**) at the back of the end zone. This is the option teams most often choose after scoring a touchdown.

Two-point conversion: When a team is trying to make a comeback or set itself up for victory in a close game, they will sometimes attempt a two-point conversion after scoring a touchdown. The two-point conversion starts with the offensive team being given the football on the two-yard line outside of their scoring end zone. The offense is then given one chance to catch the ball in, or have a ball carrier run the ball into, the end zone. If successful, they earn two points; if not, they are awarded nothing and need to kick the ball back to the other team.

Simple math will normally tell you when a team will go for a two-point conversion. For example, if one team is ahead 21–10 and the trailing team scores a touchdown to make the score 21–16, kicking an extra point will still leave them behind by four points (21–17). This would mean they can only win with a touchdown. If, however, the scoring team goes for and makes a two-point conversion, then the score becomes 21–18, which means they can tie the score with a three-point field goal to force overtime. Alternatively, if a team scores a touchdown to take the lead and make the score 19–17, they may attempt a two-point conversion (bringing the score to 21–17 if successful) to force the other team to make a touchdown to take back the lead. The key numbers to remember in football are 3, 7, and 8 because those numbers allow a team to score on one possession to either tie or win a game.

Field goal: If an offensive team gets close to the defense's end zone without scoring a touchdown, they may attempt a field goal. The play is run by the special teams and the kick is performed by the placekicker. The ball is snapped to a holder seven yards behind the line of scrimmage with the kicker needing to hit the ball between the goal posts in order to score three points for their team. A field goal is worth three points regardless of how far away it is kicked, and is often used at the end of the second quarter to add a few more points before halftime. It is also used frequently at the end of close games to tie and send them to overtime, or win when only behind by one or two points.

Safety: A safety is worth two points and can only be scored by or credited to a defense, although an offensive team can make a mistake that can lead to a safety being scored. There are three ways a defense can score a safety: (1) by tackling a ball carrier in the offense's own end zone; (2) by having the offense commit a penalty in the end zone; or (3) by having an offensive or special teams player step out of bounds in the end zone with possession of the football. Any of these will result in the defense scoring two points and the other team kicking the ball to them for an offensive possession, making it a very good play for any team who scores a safety during a game.

PENALTIES

Penalties can lose football games. One or two throughout a game may not be that big of a deal; but sloppy play can lead to penalty yards that add up and keep a team heading in the wrong direction and out of the end zone. Sometimes, a single penalty is a big deal, depending on when it happens and how many yards a team is penalized. Following are the most commonly called penalties, though there are many more you'll hear during any given broadcast.

Delay of game: We have already talked about the play clock that ticks off the seconds a team has before they are required to snap the ball and run their next play. Coming off an official's timeout or return from a commercial break, a team will be granted 25 seconds to run their play with the game's referee starting the play clock. During normal play as players are running up and down the field, the play clock is set at 40 seconds. Anytime the play clock is allowed to reach zero without a snap being made, a delay of game penalty is called on the offense. The penalty for delay of game is five yards.

False start: When an offensive player moves or even flinches before the snap, it is a false start because it makes the defense believe the play has started when it hasn't. This penalty is called immediately, the play is blown dead, and a five-yard penalty is assessed on the offense.

Offsides: When any part of a defensive player is across the line of the ball placement as the ball is snapped, they are penalized for being offsides. The game play continues and the offense has the option to take this five-yard penalty on the defense or to take the results of the play instead. This flag will also cause announcers to use the phrase **"free play"** since an offense knows that if something goes wrong, the play will be negated by the defensive penalty. You may see a defensive player actually make contact with an offensive player before the snap. This is a similar infraction that results in an immediate play stoppage and a five-yard encroachment penalty.

Offensive holding: When offensive players are blocking a defensive player, there are limitations to how they can try to control the

movement and advancement of that player. If they use techniques or blocking styles that are not allowed, it is called "holding." This is normally when the offensive player pulls a defender down to the ground or holds the outside of their shoulder pads to keep them from moving in a certain direction. When called, this is a 10-yard penalty on the offense, doubling the amount of yardage a team needs for a first down.

Defensive holding: When a defensive player grabs an offensive player running a **pass route** before the ball is in the air, it is called "defensive holding." This is a costly penalty for every defense because it comes with a five-yard penalty and an automatic first down. A nuance to this rule is that contact like grabbing can occur within the first five yards of the line of scrimmage because the offensive player may be blocking for a ball carrier on a running play.

Offensive pass interference: When an offensive player is running a pass route, they are often looking to gain an advantage against the player trying to defend them. Sometimes the receiver will make too much contact with the defense and draw an offensive pass inter-ference penalty. A common way of drawing this penalty is when the receiver "pushes off" the defense—when they see where the ball is going and push the defender in the opposite direction to create space to make the catch. This costs the offense whatever gains they made and an additional 10 yards.

Defensive pass interference: This can be the biggest of all penalties in the NFL and can have a major impact on the outcome of a game depending on when it occurs. When an offensive player is running a pass route and is physically prevented from making the catch by a defender who is not going after the football themselves, it is called "defensive pass interference." Defensive players can also be called for this penalty if they are trying to block the line of sight of an offense player without knowing where the ball is in the air or by making con-tact with one arm while going after the football with the other. This penalty results in the ball being moved to where the foul occurred and gives the offense a first down. If the penalty is called in the end zone, the offense gets the ball on the one-yard line. You can see how this can be a game-changing or momentum-changing penalty.

Roughing the passer: This penalty is called almost every time a defensive player hits the quarterback in the head or hits the quar-terback too long after they have thrown the ball downfield. It will also be called when, in the act of tackling/sacking, the defensive player lands on the quarterback with their full body weight if it was deemed possible to avoid such contact. Calls for roughing the passer are seen more often now than in years past because of an emphasis on player safety, particularly that of the quarterback. You will usually see quarterbacks, after standing back up from a sack or hard hit, ask the officials to throw the flag for this 15-yard penalty, which results in an automatic first down. Hard hits on the quarterback can get players ejected from football games and/or fined by the NFL.

Roughing the kicker: When a team is punting the ball or trying to kick a field goal, the protection of the punter or placekicker is important because their job leaves them vulnerable to injury. If a defensive player runs into a kicker's plant leg while their kicking leg is extended into the air, a roughing-the-kicker penalty will be called as they are putting that player at risk of serious and career-ending injury. Just as with roughing-the-passer penalties, the penalty is 15 yards and an automatic first down. If the contact is less severe or dangerous, such as less forcibly and unintentionally running into a kicker's kicking leg during the kick, it could result in a five-yard penalty that is not an automatic first down. If contact is made as a result of a block by a member of the kicker's team that forced the defender into the kicker, then a penalty is not called. Unless the contact was severe, there will be no penalty if the defender touches the ball when kicked.

Too many men on the field: Each team is allowed to have 11 players on the field for each play. Sometimes, while both an offensive or defensive team is making substitutions, an extra player will stay too long in the huddle or even line up with their teammates. When this happens, the play is stopped and a five-yard penalty is called. There are, however, no rules against an offense or defense running a play with ten players or less on the field.

Personal foul: A personal foul is a penalty committed by a football player that is theirs and theirs alone. It is not committed during the act of a football play, such as pass interference or offsides, but rather it's a penalty that the player who commits the infraction is called out for directly. This can be a penalty for roughing a kicker or passer or even using certain types of blocks on the field that are deemed too dangerous. All of these personal fouls are subject to a 15-yard penalty and potential player ejection. Personal fouls are common during heated divisional games when teams know each other well or when a game's score becomes lopsided and the losing team shows frustration.

Unsportsmanlike conduct: When a player is upset or angry about how a game is going or just loses their self-control, they may commit an unsportsmanlike conduct penalty. Taunting another player during or after a play or excessively celebrating after a play (sack, touchdown, interception, etc.) can also result in this penalty and the loss of 15 yards. This is also the call if a player makes excessive contact with an official. In those instances, the 15-yard penalty is assessed and the player is usually ejected and possibly suspended.

REPLAY CHALLENGES AND REVIEWS

As you watch more and more games on your high-definition flat screen television, you are bound to scream, "How did they miss that?" at the officials calling the game. We all do it, so don't be embarrassed; be proud . . . you're a real fan now!

In recent years, the NFL has allowed teams to **challenge** certain rulings made by officials during games.

When a play is deemed worthy of a challenge, an NFL head coach throws a red flag onto the field. The flag must be thrown before the ball is snapped for the next play. An official comes to their sidelines where the head coach will explain about what part of the previous play they want reviewed. The game's referee will then consult with a group of officials who are watching the game (often referred to as "being reviewed in New York") and will determine if the call was incorrect and a change needs to be made.

Every challenge situation assumes that the call on the field is correct, which means there needs to be strong enough evidence found in replay to overturn that call. If the replay shows the officials that the call on the field was correct, they will rule that the call is "confirmed." If there is not enough proof that the call was incorrect, the officials will rule that the call "stands" as originally called on the field, and play will continue. In these instances, the team who challenged the call will lose one of their time-outs for the half (meaning, also, that if a team has no time-outs, they cannot challenge any calls) and one of their two allotted replay challenges for the game.

If the replay shows that the call on the field was incorrect, the correct call will be made and the challenging team will not be charged a time-out or lose a challenge. After the two-minute warnings of both halves and during overtime, a coach cannot challenge a ruling. Designated replay officials decide on their own to review rulings during those time periods. Believe it or not, fans still see some bad calls from officials, even after these reviews!

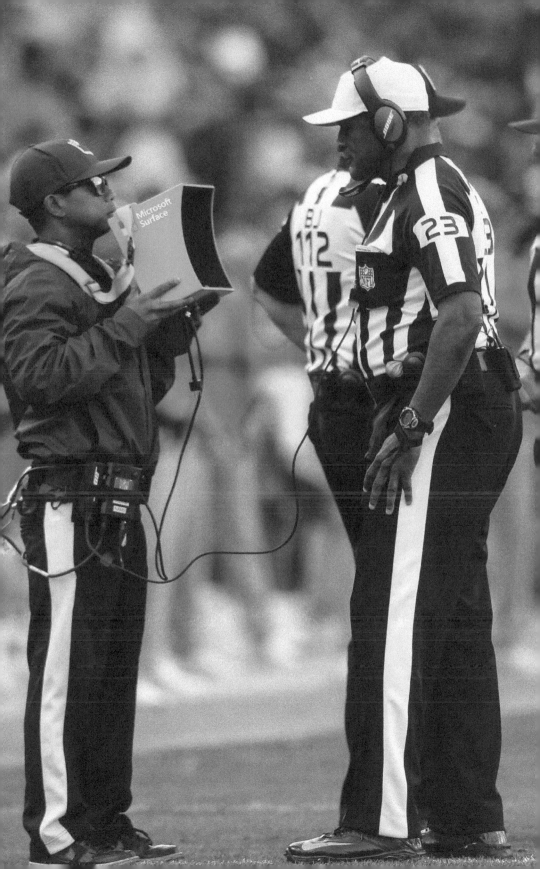

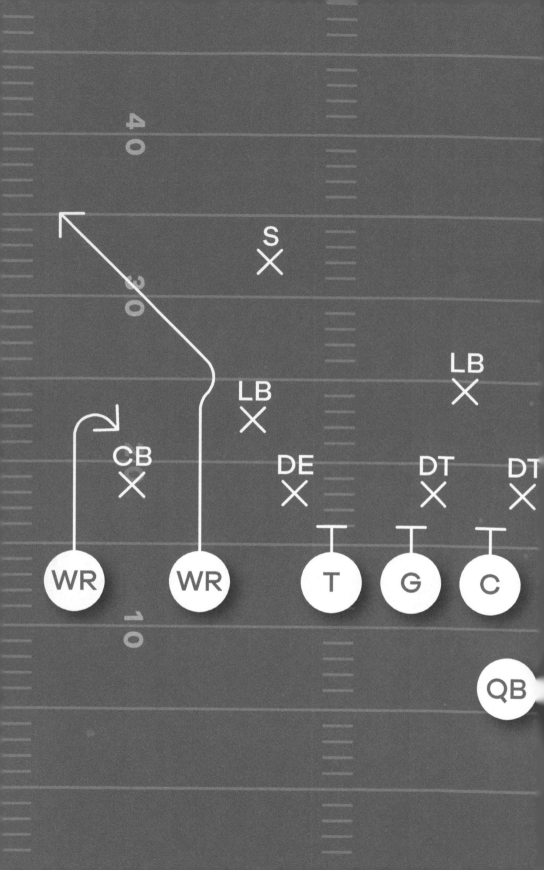

THE SPECTATOR'S PLAYBOOK

Congrats! You made it to our favorite chapter. That's right, this chapter is nothing but football plays and explanations of what goes on during those plays. This chapter will give you a clear understanding of what each player's assignment is on a given play, and what the strategy behind the play is. The offensive and defensive plays we share in this chapter are a perfect way to get your feet wet in recognizing and understanding football plays.

PLAYBOOK SYMBOLS

Bubble: Zone area

⟶ : Direction player must travel on given play

⊢ : Blocking assignment

OFFENSE ◯

QB: Quarterback

RB: Running Back

WR: Wide Receiver

TE: Tight End

C: Center

G: Guard

T: Tackle

DEFENSE ✕

DT: Defensive Tackle

DE: Defensive End

LB: Linebackers

MLB: Middle Linebacker

OLB: Outside Linebacker

CB: Cornerback

S: Safety

SPECIAL TEAMS ▢

K: Kicker

H: Holder

LS: Long Snapper

P: Punter

PR: Punt Returner

KR: Kick Returner

OFFENSIVE STRATEGIES

The number one goal of any offense in football is to score points. That is their objective and mission every time they step onto the field. Now, the offense would prefer to score a touchdown every time, but they will gladly take a field goal if a touchdown is not possible. To score a touchdown or a field goal, an offense must be able to move the ball down the field by either running or throwing the football. It is through the success of the running or passing game that the offense will be able to put themselves in position to score points.

The offense will study game film of the opposing defense to find out their weaknesses and exploit them during the game. For example, if a team watches film and sees that a defense struggles against the run game, expect that team's offense to run the ball as much as possible against them. Or, if the defense can't stop any wide receiver from catching the ball, expect the quarterback of the offense to come out slinging the ball. If you watch the NFL long enough, you will be able to determine which teams' defenses lack one or both.

QUARTERBACK STRATEGIES

The quarterback is the leader of any offense, and it is their job to communicate the play call, make sure all the players on offense are lined up correctly, and give the ball to any **eligible player** on offense that they feel can help put their team in position to score. This can be accomplished by the quarterback throwing the football, handing the football off to a running back, or keeping the ball and trying to pick up some yards (if the quarterback is fast, this option works even better).

A good quarterback is expected to watch game film—the most among the team—of every opponent and work with the offensive coordinator to formulate a solid strategy to attack a defense each game.

CATCH THE BALL

"Catch the ball" sounds simple enough, yet you will learn as you watch football that it is not always as easy as it seems. Catch the ball is when a quarterback throws the football to either a wide receiver, running back, or tight end, and the player on the receiving end of the ball is tasked with catching the football with both hands and fully securing it. From there, if possible, they try to gain more yards by running or pushing toward the opposing team's end zone.

HAND OFF THE BALL

"Hand off the ball" is a phrase that some quarterbacks, but mostly running backs, love to hear. Quarterbacks like to hand off the ball because their job in this play is essentially just giving the ball to the running back and then getting out of their way. To running backs, it means that they will be carrying the football on that offensive play and they will be tasked with gaining positive yards.

While this is arguably the easiest play for a quarterback, botched handoffs are a risk that often result in fumbles.

RUN WITH IT

"Run with it" means the quarterback runs with the football. Most times, the play called is not for a quarterback to run the ball, but rather the opportunity presents itself if receivers can't get open or the quarterback is faced with pressure by the defense. Some quarterbacks are more mobile than others and will use this option somewhat often. There are also times when the play design calls for the quarterback to run. For example, if the quarterback is fast or tough to bring down, the play is designed for the quarterback to run with it. While watching a game, you will quickly be able to identify which quarterbacks are athletic and mobile, and which aren't.

WHY DON'T QUARTERBACKS JUST RUN WITH THE BALL ON EVERY PLAY?

Every quarterback has probably dreamed about seeing a hole in the defensive line, crashing through it, and running the ball into the end zone for a touchdown. Finally, the quarterback gets to celebrate with the spike of the football! For many, though, this is just a fantasy.

Many quarterbacks are simply not fast enough to outrun even the heaviest of defenders, and some quarterbacks are terrified of getting hit when they don't have to. Think about it: Quarterbacks are already concerned about being sacked on every play; they don't want to be tackled when they don't have to be.

Another reason quarterbacks won't run the ball on every play is that they have more faith in their arm than their legs, and for good reason. Quarterbacks are trained to throw accurate passes to their offensive weapons, and they know they can pick up way more yards if they are successful at throwing.

There are some fast and mobile quarterbacks that a coach can incorporate into their running game plan. You might see those quarterbacks carrying the ball more often at the risk of injury on every one of those plays. So this strategy must be carefully considered so as to not overuse or lose the quarterback.

HOW TO READ OFFENSIVE PLAYS

Offensive plays can seem confusing at first, but they'll be easy to read once we break it down. For starters, when reading an offensive play, you want to be able to locate and determine which positions will be involved. You usually have a quarterback, running back, wide receivers, tight ends, and offensive linemen making up the play. (The symbols on page 72 are a great guide to pinpoint which players will be on the field for a play.)

When reading a play in the following illustrations, you want to pay attention to the direction the arrows are pointing regarding the wide receivers and running backs. This is important because it tells the direction their route will go. There is usually a line pointing forward with a second line going across that points the offensive linemen in the direction of their blocking assignments. You may see wide receivers, running backs, and tight ends with a similar line directing them to move forward and then stop at a blocking assignment if the play calls for them to block instead of run. You will be able to determine if the play is a run or pass by looking at the blocking assignments of the different players.

OFF-TACKLE

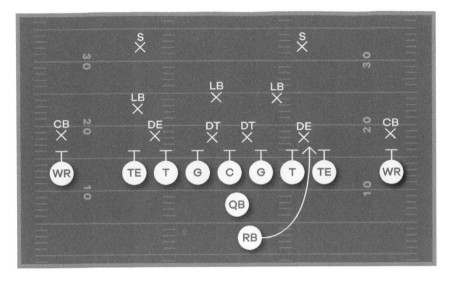

An off-tackle run play is when the running back carries the foot-ball through a running lane that was provided by the tackle's block. Often, there may be a fullback used to lead the running back through the hole to provide extra blocking. The fullback is usually tasked with blocking either the middle linebacker or the safety during the play. This is one of the most used plays in football and, if performed cor-rectly, it can lead to many positive yards.

In the illustration, the C snaps the ball to the QB, who hands it off to the RB lined up directly behind him. The RB runs to his right, anticipating that the T and TE have made a lane for him by blocking the defensive players from entering his running path.

JET SWEEP

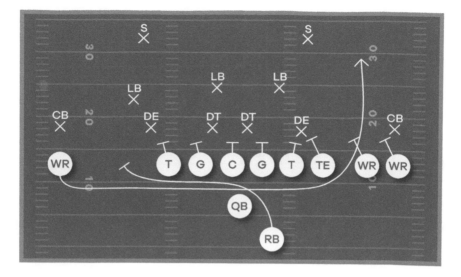

A jet sweep play is a running play in which the quarterback takes the snap and hands the ball off to a wide receiver that is in motion from one side of the field to the other. Usually, the wide receiver that is receiving the handoff is fast enough to outrun the initial defensive linemen attempting to make a tackle behind the line of scrimmage.

In the illustration, the C will snap the ball to the QB, who will hand the ball off to the WR as he moves horizontally across the field. If the offense is successful in blocking the defensive players, the WR with the ball can cut up the field toward the end zone.

The danger of a jet sweep play is the potential for the ball carrier to be tackled for no gain or a loss of yards because the carrier is initially running horizontally before cutting up the field.

POST PATTERN

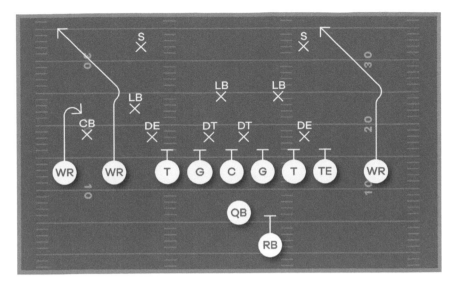

A post pattern play is a passing play in which the receivers run deep down the field and then angle their routes toward the goal post. This is a deep passing play that can pick up several yards if successfully completed.

In the illustration, the C will snap the ball to the QB, who will back up and scan the field looking for which WR is open to receive a throw. (You may hear announcers speaking about "football IQ," which is knowledge of the game and being able to read a field. Quarterbacks with a high football IQ are more successful on plays like this because they're able to anticipate what the opposing defense is doing and work around it.)

As with any deep passing play, the danger in a play like this is in waiting for it to develop. The quarterback must stand in the pocket and wait for his receiver to get down the field to throw it, which opens the quarterback up to potential sacking if the play takes too long.

PLAY-ACTION PASS

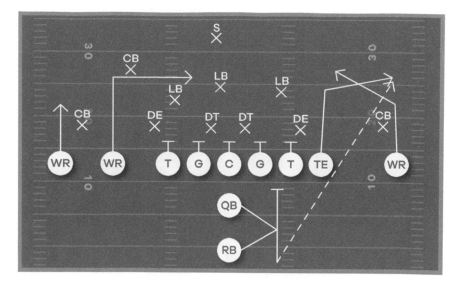

A play-action pass play is when the quarterback fakes a handoff to the running back before throwing the football to any receiving option. The fake makes defenders momentarily stop because they believe a run is upcoming. Most play-action plays are successful when the offense has a strong running attack that the defense needs to be constantly aware of and ready to respond to.

In the illustration, the C will snap the ball to the QB who will fake a handoff to the RB lined up directly behind him. While the RB pretends to have the ball and runs a route, the QB will move back and scan the field for an open WR.

The danger of play-action plays is that they usually take a bit of time to develop, which could lead to the quarterback getting sacked before they throw the football.

SCREEN PLAY

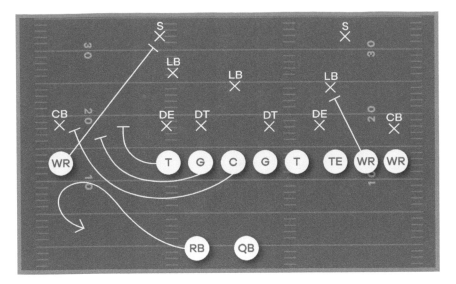

A screen play is when a group of players on offense set up a coordinated wall of blockers, or a "screen," enabling the player receiving the football to gain yards. To give the players time to set up the block, the pass is usually short and thrown behind the line of scrimmage. Most of the time, members of the offensive line run out to provide the blocking for the screen play, while the running back or wide receiver receives the football.

In the illustration, the C will snap the ball to the QB, who will hand the ball off to the RB or throw a short pass to a WR, while the offense sets up the screen against the defense.

The danger of a screen play is that it needs time to set up, and for much of that time the quarterback is completely open to be hit.

DEFENSIVE STRATEGIES

The main goal of any defense in football is to stop the offense in their tracks and get them off the field without any points scored. That is easier said than done, but good defense makes it happen on a consistent basis. Tackling well, providing good coverage that makes it hard for receivers to catch the ball, and having the ability to put pressure on the quarterback are all basic defensive strategies that can help a defense achieve their goal.

Just like the offense, a defense studies game film of opposing offenses to identify their weaknesses (for example, if an offense is terrible at protecting their quarterback or if the wide receivers are inconsistent in catching), so the defense can exploit them during the game. Though it may be counterintuitive, you may hear announcers say that "defense wins games," and they're speaking from experience.

TACKLING

Tackling is one of the basic functions that all defensive players must know how to do correctly. If a defensive player can tackle the ball carrier, he is able to stop or limit him from gaining yards. Tackling is extremely important to a good defense, yet there are players that struggle with it. There are good tackling techniques and bad ones. In its most simple terms, a good tackle involves wrapping up the ball carrier and bringing them to the ground.

PLAYING COVERAGE

Playing good **coverage**—guarding receivers so they can't catch the ball—is essential to the success of any defense. This job mostly falls on cornerbacks tasked with covering receivers, though there are times when safeties and linebackers can go into coverage. Some people say covering receivers is one of the hardest things to do in football, which is why most people would also say cornerback is the hardest position to play, right behind playing quarterback. When covering a receiver, who is usually quite fast, a player must follow that receiver all over the field and prevent him from catching the ball. It sounds simple, but this is extremely hard, especially when there are no clues as to which way a receiver will go or the sudden movements they will make to shed the defender and get open. Playing coverage is also when many penalties happen, such as holding or pass interference.

PRESSURING THE QUARTERBACK

If you can get pressure on a quarterback, you can shut down a quarterback, and thus shut down an offense. A defense can pressure a quarterback with the defensive line pushing the offensive line back, or they can do so through blitzing. Now, blitzing is cool because it involves sending multiple defensive players—more than the offensive blockers can handle—to rush the quarterback. For example, safeties, linebackers, and even cornerbacks can team up to try to get to the quarterback when a defense decides to blitz.

Good defenses know that getting continual, solid pressure on a quarterback will lead to mistakes and possibly a win.

-- FOOTBALL FAQ --
IS DEFENSE MORE IMPORTANT THAN OFFENSE?

Yes, defense is more important than offense. One thousand times, YES (subjectively, of course)! Don't get it wrong, offense is important, but defense is far more critical to a team winning or losing. Think about it: A good defense can overcome a good offense, and if the defense is exceptional, it can score off an offense. That means you are getting two for the price of one with an exceptional defense, which you can't get with a good or great offense that can only score. A reminder of the obvious: The team that scores the most points wins the game. If a defense can keep

Continued >>

the opponent from scoring, it takes the pressure off of their own offensive players.

Look at some of the previous great teams in NFL history: the '70s Pittsburgh Steelers (the Steel Curtain), the '85 Chicago Bears (Monsters of the Midway), and the '13 Seattle Seahawks (Legion of Boom). All these great teams had amazing defenses (with legendary nicknames) leading them to victory. So, if anyone ever asks you which is more important, offense or defense, always go with defense, and impress them with your knowledge of football monikers.

HOW TO READ DEFENSIVE PLAYS

Reading defensive plays isn't too different from reading offensive plays. Sure, the symbols may be a little different from offensive plays (for reference, check out defensive play symbols on page 72), but you will find there are similarities between the two. One difference to point out is that there are sometimes bubbles within defensive plays that symbolize areas a player must occupy and defend during a play. This is usually shown during **zone coverage** plays, where a player covers a particular area of the field. The other type of defensive play is man coverage, where players defend and follow a particular offensive player regardless of where that player goes on the field.

COVER 0

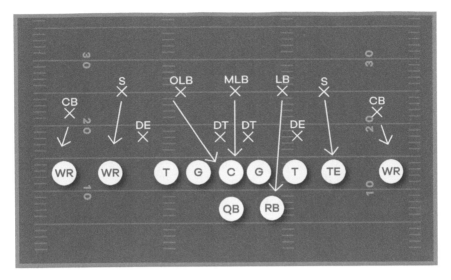

Cover 0 is straight up man-to-man coverage. There are no deep safeties because the safeties are nearer to the line of scrimmage and likely covering a player or blitzing to disrupt the play or sack the quarterback. Also, if you haven't figured it out yet, it is called "Cover 0" because there are zero deep safeties.

The danger of cover 0 is that there is no underneath help for the cornerbacks. This means that if a cornerback gets beat, the opposing player has the potential to go for many yards, if not a touchdown.

PREVENT DEFENSE

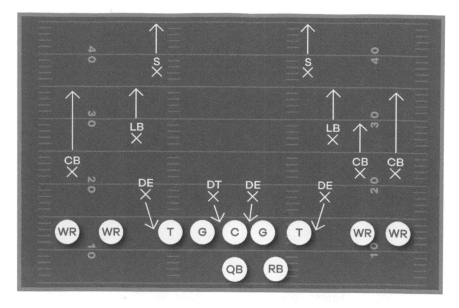

Prevent defense is the defensive formation employed when the defense is trying to prevent any long passes. This means the cornerbacks, safeties, and sometimes even the linebackers are 10 to 20 yards from the line of scrimmage.

The danger of a prevent defense is that a team is conceding easy yardage on short passes or running plays, and if there is enough time, the driving team could potentially get in position to score. You will likely see a prevent defense when a defense suspects the opponent of attempting a **Hail Mary** pass before halftime or at the end of a game.

COVER 1

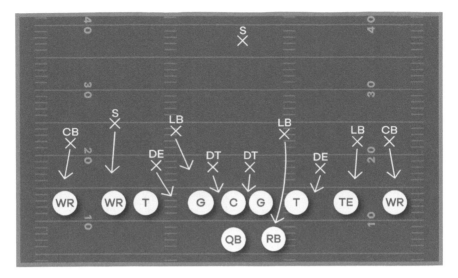

Cover 1 is a man-to-man coverage among all the **defensive backs**. However, there is one player (usually a safety) that remains back to provide deep support. If you noticed, this play is like cover 0; the only difference is that one player remains back, which is where the "cover 1" name comes from.

The danger of cover 1 is that there is only one player providing deep support; thus an offense can exploit it if multiple receivers run deep routes and beat the players defending them man-to-man.

COVER 2

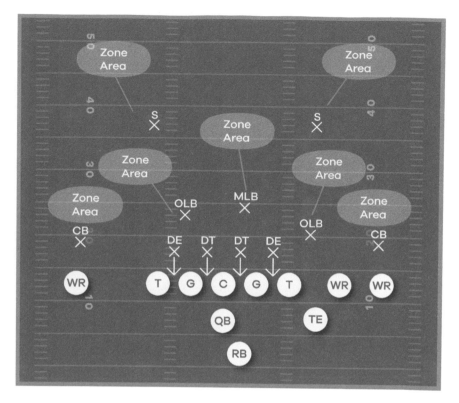

Cover 2 is a zone defensive coverage. All the defensive backs and linebackers in this coverage must defend an area or "zone" of the field. The two safeties play deep and each cover half of the football field. These two areas are called over-the-top zones. The cornerbacks and linebackers defend areas in between the line of scrimmage and the over-the-top zones (this area is broken down into five underneath zones).

The danger of cover 2 is that a good quarterback can pick apart the coverage, since there are bound to be holes within the defense. For example, a player must man an area of the field in zone coverage, but what happens if a receiver finds an area that isn't manned, or waits in an area in between zones, causing confusion as to which defensive player should defend him? It's an easy answer: The offense gains positive yards.

ZONE BLITZ

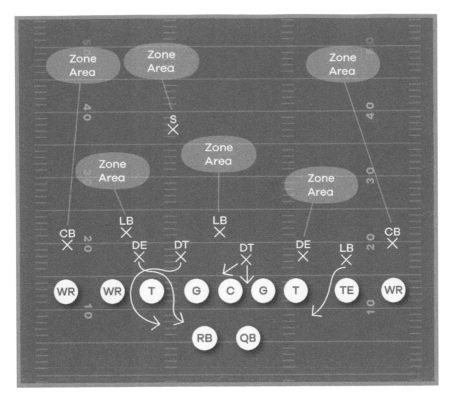

Zone blitz is a defensive play designed to rush the passer while dropping one of the defensive lineman into coverage to confuse the offensive line as well as the quarterback. This type of play also calls for zone defense. This means that the cornerbacks, safeties, and designated linebackers each cover an area or "zone" of the field.

The danger of a zone blitz play is the mismatch created by the defensive lineman who has dropped back in coverage. If a quarterback realizes that a defensive lineman, who is generally not as fast nor as agile, is in pass coverage, he could target him and make that lineman a liability. Also, zone blitz plays usually perform poorly against running plays, since a lineman leaves a vacancy on the line when he drops into pass coverage.

WHEN SHOULD NFL TEAMS "GO FOR IT" ON FOURTH DOWN?

One of the difficult decisions every NFL head coach faces during the season is when his offense should attempt to go for a first down when it is fourth down. The first consideration is where the offense is on the field when they face fourth down. Generally speaking, the closer a team is to their own end zone (the end zone behind them), the less likely they are to attempt a fourth down play. They do not want to give the ball up to the opponent so close to scoring position if their fourth down attempt is unsuccessful.

Toward the end of the first half (second quarter), with too little time remaining for the other team to attempt a play, is one time when going for it on fourth down may be considered safe. Another safe option would be toward the end of the game, when there's not enough time on the clock to have another possession, and they need to score points to secure a tie or win.

This decision often depends on many factors. One of them might be how well the opposing team's defense is playing. For example, if an offense has been having success against the opposing defense all game and easily driving the ball down the field, the decision to go for it would likely be an easy one. However, if the defense has been successful, making consistent stops against the offense the entire game, there may be some hesitation for the offense to go for it.

Another consideration is the opposing quarterback. If a team is facing a quarterback like Patrick Mahomes or Aaron Rodgers, both known for winning late in the game with very little time on the clock, going for a fourth down might be considered the best way to keep them off the field, or it may be considered too risky for a head coach to try because coming up short might mean a nearly certain loss.

Unless you have a vested interest in the outcome, it can be quite funny to watch fans during a heated moment of a game when the coach decides to go for it on fourth down. You can just listen to the team's fans to know whether the play was successful or not. "That was a brilliant call!" or "Why didn't we just punt?" The celebration or complaining will tell you all you need to know about the outcome.

FANTASTIC MOMENTS IN FOOTBALL

The journey is almost over, and we will soon have to let you out into the world. Don't worry, though; if you made it this far, you're ready for some football! In our final chapter, we'll give you a little taste of the rich history of professional American football. We'll talk about some of the most memorable moments by some of the best players in NFL history, and some of the most fantastic games that have taken place, including the biggest of all games. Think of this chapter as a two-point conversion: You're good to watch football, but why not go for more (talking) points?

FAMOUS GAMES

The NFL has seen many memorable games during its history, many of which were captured by television cameras, allowing generations of fans who weren't alive at the time to view these moments. Here are a few such games that come to mind:

ICE BOWL (1967)

One of the most famous NFL games also happened to be one of the coldest. The 1967 NFL Championship pit the Dallas Cowboys against the Green Bay Packers in a game that went down in infamy. The game was played on Lambeau Field with temperatures below -13°F at kickoff. The Packers started off with a 14-0 lead, but the extreme temperature began to affect the Packers, causing them to fumble twice and allowing the Cowboys to get back into the game. By half-time, the Cowboys had managed to cut the Packers lead to 14-10. It wasn't until the fourth quarter that the Cowboys took a 17-14 lead over the Packers with less than 5 minutes remaining. However, the Packers had legendary quarterback Bart Starr, who drove down the field and had the team within inches of scoring. With no timeouts left and having been stopped on back-to-back run plays, legendary Packers coach Vince Lombardi made the call to go for the touchdown and the win (as opposed to tying the game with a field goal), and Starr decided to call his own number, diving for the end zone and scoring to seal the Packers victory.

EPIC IN MIAMI (1981)

The AFC Divisional game between the San Diego (now Los Angeles) Chargers and the Miami Dolphins was a legendary battle that still gets fans talking today. The Chargers jumped out to a 24-0 lead on the road, yet Miami turned the game around in the second quarter with its defense by not allowing a single point. Miami's offense posted 17 points to bring the score within seven. By the end of the third quarter, the score was tied at 31 as the feverish pace of the game began to take its toll on the players. In the fourth quarter, the teams swapped touchdowns, forcing the game into overtime to decide a winner. Exhausted from the heat and humidity, and with more than 1,000 yards of offense in the record books, the Chargers finally kicked a field goal to win a game that marked a change in how NFL football was played. From this game forward, the league slowly changed the rules, making it easier to give fans what they enjoyed seeing: players being athletic on the field and high-scoring games. For example, they modified the rules regarding physical contact on passing plays, making it more likely a penalty was called if a defensive player contacted an offensive player while the pass was still in the air. This change made it easier for wide receivers to catch passes, gain more yards, and for teams to score more points.

"THE CATCH" NFC CHAMPIONSHIP GAME (1980 SEASON)

This game featured a prominent team of the 1970s, the Dallas Cowboys, against the upstart San Francisco 49ers. It not only earned a nickname but ushered in a new era in the NFL, as the "West Coast Offense" became as well-known as the run-pass option of the 21st century.

Down by six points to the Dallas Cowboys, San Francisco 49ers quarterback Joe Montana led his team down the field and was in position to send his team to The Big Game. It was third and four on the Dallas 6-yard line with 51 seconds left in the game. After the snap, Montana was chased out of the pocket and, looking to avoid a sack, he tossed the ball toward the back of the end zone. Despite looking like the ball was overthrown and headed to the seats, it was caught by 49ers tight end Dwight Clark for the touchdown, sending his team to their first championship game (which they would go on to win).

The play, nicknamed "The Catch" (the NFL does love its nicknames), marked a changing of the guard in the NFC as the Dallas Cowboys took a decade to return to their winning ways and the San Francisco 49ers became a dynasty of the 1980s, winning four championships during the decade. To this day there is discussion as to whether Montana was aiming for Clark or just trying to throw the ball away.

HOW DOES THE NFL ENCOURAGE DRAMATIC ENDINGS TO GAMES?

Week after week and season after season, the NFL rulebook helps facilitate dramatic endings to many games. One of the ways they do this is with some rules that help teams come back from behind, score, and either tie or win the game at the end of the fourth quarter.

One of the most-used rules that helps teams when they are trying to score late in a game applies when a player goes out of bounds. During most of the game, when a ball carrier goes out of bounds, officials place the ball at the line of scrimmage for the offense, and the clock will begin counting down again. However, when there are less than two minutes left in the fourth quarter, the game clock stops and won't start again until the next play begins. This rule saves time for the team trying to score before the game ends and helps create dramatic endings. And it keeps us tuned in to the game—you know we love drama at the end of games.

Another way the NFL encourages dramatic endings is through the **onside kick**. This is a play that teams can use after they score to try and get the ball back: When they are supposed to kickoff as far as possible to give possession back to the other team, instead, they kick it short and try to grab it before the other team does. If they succeed, they gain possession and can try to score again. The key rule to an onside kick is that the ball does need to advance at least 10 yards before the kicking team can recover, so it isn't as if the kicker can just kick it to his own player nearby. If they touch it before it travels that distance, it is a penalty and a re-kick. The play is extremely difficult to execute in a game and largely unsuccessful, so it's usually only called in times of desperation.

FAMOUS MOMENTS

NFL games are often a series of moments strung together that create lasting memories—some amazing, some heart-breaking, depending on your team.

"TUCK RULE" AFC DIVISIONAL PLAYOFFS (2001 SEASON)

When it comes to famous moments, few compare to the "Tuck Rule" play between the Oakland (now Las Vegas) Raiders and the New England Patriots. The game was a 2001 AFC Divisional playoff game played in the snow of Foxboro Stadium (Patriots' home stadium) in January 2002.

The snow had been the story for most of the game as it kept both teams from scoring as much as they could have, but Mother Nature took a backseat to the rulebook late in the fourth quarter. With the Raiders leading 13–10, cornerback Charles Woodson blitzed Patriots quarterback Tom Brady and, at first glance, forced a fumble from his fellow Michigan alum. (Even many fans of Brady thought it was a fumble and that the game was over.) The game officials, however, citing a rule introduced in 1999, ruled that Brady's throwing arm was moving forward, thus making the fumble an incomplete pass and denying the Raiders possession and the win. (Sorry, Raiders fans.)

New England went on to tie the game with a field goal and kicked another field goal in overtime to secure the win. This game was part of a magical run that Tom Brady and the New England Patriots began in the snow that night.

"THE FUMBLE" AFC CHAMPIONSHIP GAME (1987 SEASON)

In the late 1980s, two AFC teams dueled for conference supremacy: the Denver Broncos and the Cleveland Browns. One of those games provided a moment still talked about decades later as one in which neither team deserved to lose and how one team falling short reads like a Greek tragedy.

The visiting Broncos went to Cleveland and jumped out to an early 14–0 lead in the first quarter. They held a halftime lead of 21–3, and saw the scoreboard read 28–10 in the third quarter. Fed by the fans in Cleveland's stadium (the "Dawg Pound"), Cleveland players did not give up, and would eventually tie the game at 31–31 before Denver's John Elway drove for one more touchdown, making the score 38–31 late in the fourth quarter. Drawing on their fans one more time, the Browns drove the ball inside the Denver 10-yard line and looked poised to tie the score and send the game to overtime. However, on a draw play, Cleveland running back Earnest Byner fumbled the ball inside the five, giving possession to the Broncos—handing them the AFC title, and a trip to The Big Game.

"ONE YARD SHORT," SUPER BOWL XXXIV (1999 SEASON)

With a score of 23–16, Super Bowl XXXIV between the St. Louis Rams and Tennessee Titans would come down to the final play. Down by seven, on the Rams 10-yard line, and with only five seconds on the clock, Tennessee quarterback Steve McNair found

wide receiver Kevin Dyson who caught the ball on a short **slant** from the six-yard line; but Rams' linebacker Mike Jones tackled him just short of the end zone, and the clock reached 0:00, giving St. Louis the win. The play was called "One Yard Short" and images of Dyson desperately trying to stretch the ball into the end zone are still shown as one of the most dramatic endings in history. We imagine Titans fans are still stinging from that final play (we would be) and knowing they were literally one yard from having the chance to win a championship.

Football Traditions

Football is rich with traditions as each team and its fan base is often best known for one particular thing they do or bring with them to the game. Fans, too, have their way of supporting their team, even if they are watching from home, with some of their traditions rooted in superstition. Players pay homage to the history of the team they play for, with fans in the stands always willing to keep the traditions alive, week after week and generation after generation.

Begun as a way to support the team during the 1975 NFL Playoffs, fans of the Pittsburgh Steelers are known for waving their "Terrible Towels" in the stands. The yellow towels with the black Steelers name written on them were once as feared as the Steel Curtain defense of the 1970s and are still a symbol of a proud fan base.

Regardless of what city the Raiders franchise calls home, their fans have often had a section of seats behind one of the end zones dubbed "The Black Hole." This is where fans dress in all black attire and costumes such as Darth Vader, an evil pirate, or a fearsome motorcycle rider in an effort to intimidate visiting players. The Star Wars theme was taken a step further when the team moved from Oakland to Las Vegas and their new home was nicknamed "The Death Star" after the Empire's battle station in the early movies.

Continued >>

Fans who are enjoying the game at home are also likely to have traditions and superstitions. Many will wear the same jersey if their team is on a winning streak, while insisting on sitting in the same seat they have been in during the streak. Buying a player's jersey is also a tradition for some fans. For example, you might purchase a jersey when a quarterback, running back, or pass rusher is drafted by your team with the hope that they become the team's next star. If they do become a star, that jersey is now "lucky" to you.

Players also have their own traditions when it comes to playing games. A nationally known one is the "Lambeau Leap," the traditional leap into the stands that a Green Bay Packers player does after scoring a touchdown at home. Other players usually just toss or throw the football into the stands, making for a happy fan, or they will keep the football for their own trophy case, especially when the score is a milestone for them. Once you start watching a team with regularity, you'll start to recognize each player's traditions and learn to expect them.

GREATEST PLAYERS

With more than 20,000 athletes donning NFL uniforms over the years, the game has seen some elite talent take the field. Even among those in the Pro Football Hall of Fame, there are a handful of players who stand out. That means there are players even the all-time greats are in awe of, just as much as fans are. Here is our list of the top five best players in NFL history.

QUARTERBACK TOM BRADY

When it comes to results on the field, few, if any, quarterbacks in NFL history can match what Tom Brady accomplished during his NFL career. The one-time Michigan Wolverine has won more championships than any other player in history, picking up more MVP awards than any other player along the way. Brady built on the legacy he already had when, after spending two decades and winning six championships with the New England Patriots, he signed as a free agent with the Tampa Bay Buccaneers and won championship number seven during his first season there. Though he may not be the most talented quarterback in NFL history—there is always a debate about individual stats, with players like Aaron Rodgers, Peyton Manning, and Joe Montana in the mix—his pages of achievements in the record books have secured Tom Brady's place in NFL history.

WIDE RECEIVER JERRY RICE

Any list of great NFL players should include the game's greatest wide receiver, Jerry Rice. (Some may say this title belongs to Randy Moss, and while Moss was amazing and this list is subjective, Jerry Rice is the correct answer.) Rice joined the NFL out of Mississippi Valley State University and played 16 of his 20 seasons with the San Francisco 49ers (with his other four played mostly with the Oakland Raiders and a very short stint with the Seattle Seahawks before retiring). He became the first NFL player to score 200 career touchdowns and was named to the NFL All-1980s and All-1990s teams while he put up league-best and record-breaking receiving stats almost every season. Even at ages 39 and 40, Rice put up 1,000-plus-yard seasons on his way to the Hall of Fame and earned the title of the greatest wide receiver in history. Rice formed a foundation to help children and families that he continues to run in his retirement, and he also serves as the honorary chairperson of the 49ers Foundation.

RUNNING BACK WALTER PAYTON

Among running backs, one of the greatest was Walter Payton of the Chicago Bears. Nicknamed "Sweetness" for his kind and generous ways both on and off the football field, Payton played college at Jackson State University before being drafted by the Bears in 1975. The team lost during Payton's first two seasons; something they had been doing since their last championship in 1963. In 1977, the Bears went 9–5 and Payton was named the Most Valuable Player as well as the NFL's Man of the Year for his charity work and community leadership. It was in 1984 when Payton made headlines as he passed the Cleveland Browns' Jim Brown to become the NFL's all-time leading rusher. The following season the Chicago Bears dominated the league and won Super Bowl XX 46–10, giving a championship ring to one of the greatest players and people to ever play. Sadly, Payton died in November 1999 from a rare liver disease, but the NFL honors his legacy annually by handing out the Walter Payton Man of the Year award to those who give back off the field.

DEFENSIVE LINEMAN REGGIE WHITE

When we think about all-time great defensive players, the first name that comes to mind is Reggie White. The "Minister of Defense" started his pro football career in the United States Football League (USFL) before embarking on his Hall of Fame NFL career with the Philadelphia Eagles. The versatile lineman led the NFL in sacks during the 1987 season, earning the star Defensive Player of the Year honors in just his third season in the league.

White, one of the first highly sought-after free agents, made headlines after joining the Green Bay Packers for the 1993 season. Four years later, White would win a long coveted championship title, and at the age of 38 in 1998, White would win a second Defense Player of the Year Award after posting 16 sacks. When leaving the NFL, Reggie White's 198 sacks were the most in history; White recorded more sacks than games played in Philadelphia and retired with more sacks than anyone in Packers' history. Sadly, White died in December 2004, one week after turning 43, too soon to be eligible for the Pro Football Hall of Fame, in which White was enshrined as part of the Class of 2006.

CORNERBACK DEION SANDERS

There are few players who cause free agent bidding wars in the NFL like Deion Sanders did. Bouncing back and forth between the San Francisco 49ers and Dallas Cowboys, the shutdown cornerback was a symbol of power for the two franchises who dueled on the field for an appearance at The Big Game and off the field for Sanders' services. Athletic enough to play a baseball and football game on the same weekend in Atlanta, Sanders defined what a shutdown cornerback was, often taking away a team's best wide receiver for most, if not the entirety, of a game, or, as Sanders often did, running the opposite way after making an interception. "Primetime" was known for more than what took place on the field; but you can't fake your way to the Pro Football Hall of Fame, where Sanders' career took him before becoming a broadcaster and then a college head coach. Deion Sanders was a one-of-a-kind player who was fun to watch and listen to as he shared his take on football from a physical and mental aspect.

LEGENDARY CHAMPIONSHIP GAMES

Because of the fanfare and prestige of the championship game, every game is memorable for one reason or another. However, some stand out for the brilliant football that was played between both teams and the heart that the players showed during the game.

SUPER BOWL III (1968 SEASON)

Although it was the third championship game between the now-defunct AFL and NFL, Super Bowl III was the first to be referred to by this title. The NFL had won the first two championship games, with the Green Bay Packers defeating the Kansas City Chiefs and Oakland Raiders after the 1966 and 1967 seasons respectively, and it was commonly thought that the AFL teams were simply less talented than the NFL teams. As such, it made perfect sense that the Baltimore Colts from the NFL were heavily favored against the upstart New York Jets, champions of the American Football League. So when the Jets, led by quarterback Joe Namath (who guaranteed a win—yeah, players were overconfident even in the '60s), beat the Colts 16–7, it shocked the entire football nation!

SUPER BOWL XXXVI

When it comes to legendary championship games, we should include the first victory of the player who has won the most football championship rings and is widely considered one of the greatest quarterbacks of all time. The game was Super Bowl XXXVI and pitted the St. Louis Rams, known as "The Greatest Show on Turf," against a New England Patriots team led by quarterback Tom Brady, who started the season as the Patriots' backup.

The Rams were the NFC Champions and a 14-point favorite over the AFC Champion Patriots who were on a Cinderella-type run, surviving the famous "Tuck Rule" game (see page 97) on their way to The Big Game. Led by Hall of Fame quarterback Kurt Warner, St. Louis expected their high-powered offense to smother the New England team that lacked star power and firepower. It was Warner, however, who gave the Patriots hope, when in the second quarter, he threw a pick-six, giving New England a 7–3 lead. Tom Brady would add a late touchdown pass to give his team a 14–3 advantage at the half.

The game stayed close in the second half, with New England only able to manage a third quarter field goal before the Rams offense finally kicked into gear. With two fourth-quarter touchdowns, the Rams tied the game at 17–17 with just 90 seconds left on the game clock, setting up what would have been a championship to be decided in overtime. One problem though: New England wasn't playing for an overtime face-off, they were playing for the win. With famed commentator and Hall of Fame coach John Madden in the booth calling for the Patriots to run out the clock, Tom Brady and the Patriots drove into Rams territory, and on the game's final play, kicker Adam Vinatieri sent a game-winning 48-yard field goal through the uprights, giving New England their first ever champion-ship game win.

What fans didn't know at the time was the Patriots were about to embark on a 20-year dynasty that saw them win six championship games in nine tries. Super Bowl XXXVI was a legendary game at the time and would be known as a benchmark in NFL history.

SUPER BOWL XXV

One of the most famous championship game moments is talked about because of someone's failure, not their success. Super Bowl XXV saw the New York Giants take on the Buffalo Bills. The Bills were an offensive machine during the 1990 season, scoring at will against most opponents, and were favored to do so again against the Giants. But the New York Giants took control of the game with a run-first offense, controlling the ball for two-thirds of the game's 60 minutes of play. Yet, despite that, Buffalo had a chance to win the game late on a 47-yard field goal attempt. For fans of the Bills, however, the ending was bitter as the kick sailed wide right and the Giants won the game 20–19, giving the NFL a famous moment at the expense of kicker Scott Norwood. Nicknamed "Wide Right," the play would be analyzed in-depth and found to have possibly been the fault of the holder Frank Reich, who lined up the ball incorrectly.

Little did fans in Buffalo know that this would be the start of four consecutive losses in The Big Game. They would reach the next three championship games but get blown out in each of them, making people wonder how much Norwood's missed kick played into their future failures.

SUPER BOWL LI

Some call this championship game the greatest game ever, while some call it the greatest comeback ever. This game had everything: two excellent quarterbacks, playmakers on both sides, and tons of drama. Super Bowl LI had the New England Patriots facing off against the Atlanta Falcons to end the 2016 NFL season. It had future Hall of Fame quarterback, Tom Brady, going for his record fifth championship ring, while NFL MVP quarterback, Matt Ryan, was attempting to win his first.

The game started off slow until the Atlanta Falcons kicked things into high gear and scored three touchdowns in the second quarter, while the Patriots could only muster a field goal. Thus, the Falcons went into halftime with a lead of 21–3.

After halftime the Falcons scored another touchdown, leading many people (including us) to believe the Falcons were just the better team and were set to run away with the game in blowout fashion. However, the Patriots had Tom Brady, and if you know anything about Tom Brady you know a lead is never safe when he is on the other sideline.

Long story short, the New England Patriots and Tom Brady rallied from being down 28–3 midway through the third quarter to tying the game and forcing overtime (we know, legendary stuff). Then, Tom Brady drove his team down the field with the first possession of overtime to win the game and mark the biggest comeback in the championship game's history.

This game is the reason the phrase "28–3" is now considered taboo to all Falcons fans, and humorous to everyone else.

College Football

If you're enjoying the game of football, you are not limited to watching the NFL. College football is nearly as popular as the pro game and is played during the same time of year. While the professional players take to the field on Sundays (and Mondays and Thursdays, but you get the point), one can watch college football for hours on Saturday afternoons every fall, with the best games scheduled for the late afternoon and in primetime. Many media outlets, such as ESPN, provide full coverage of college football, and air dozens of games across their family of networks. In recent years, smaller conferences have been highlighted during the week, making college football a seven-day-a-week sport.

Many of the rules in college and professional football are the same, though some are different to make the game easier for those who are still in school and younger than those in the NFL. However, most fans of either brand of football can enjoy the other, with many parts of the country treating their local college team as their pro franchise in the way they attend games and support the program. (You haven't seen fan support until you have witnessed college football in the South or Midwest.)

Continued >>

Most of the best college football programs are part of the Big Five: five conferences regionally situated throughout the country. These conferences are the Atlantic Coast Conference (ACC), centered on the country's East Coast; the Big Ten, primarily located in the northern Midwest; the Southeastern Conference (SEC), with their teams on the Gulf of Mexico and in the Deep South; the Big 12 Conference, which runs north and south in the nation's heartland; and the Pacific-12 Conference (Pac-12), with all their teams on or near the West Coast of the United States.

It is these schools that often produce the players drafted by pro teams in the early rounds of the NFL Draft and thus the teams most closely followed by pro fans. Those who cover college football will often tell you how these players will perform on "the next level," meaning the NFL.

GLOSSARY

There are many key terms in football; however, these terms are the ones anyone new to watching football *must* know in order to truly understand the basics of the game.

Backfield: The portion of the offense that is behind the line of scrimmage, often where running backs line up.

Blitz: When the defense sends more players than they have on their defensive line to go after the quarterback during a passing play.

Block: When an offensive player moves or gets in the way of a defensive player, making it difficult for the defense to tackle the ball carrier.

Bye: A team's off week during the regular season or between the end of the regular season and the start of the playoffs.

Challenge: The act of telling the officials on the field that the previous play might have been called incorrectly, forcing the replay official to make the final call.

Change of possession: When the team who did not have the ball at the start of a play has the ball when the play is over.

Clock management: The ability to effectively use timeouts or run the clock out at the end of the first half or the game. Coaches need to use their timeouts wisely to ensure they can stop the clock when needed, and players need to be aware not to execute plays in ways that would result in the clock stopping (for example by running out of bounds) if they need to keep the clock moving.

Collective bargaining agreement (CBA): The agreement between the NFL and the Players Association governing the basic rules of the game and the business of the sport.

Dead ball: The period of time after the whistle blows ending each play and before the ball is snapped to start the next play.

Defense: The team without possession of the ball trying to stop the team with the football.

Defensive back: The defenders that guard the wide receivers or play far away from the line of scrimmage to prevent long plays and points scored by the offense.

Defer: Choosing to take possession of the ball to start the second half after winning the coin toss.

Downs: One of four attempts to obtain the necessary yardage for the offense to maintain possession of the football.

Eligible player: A player who would be allowed to catch a forward pass based upon how an offense lines up at the snap of the football.

End zone: The 10 yards at each end of a football field where teams score touchdowns.

Extra point: A kicking play that is run after a touchdown that, if successful, adds one point to a team's score.

False start: When an offensive player moves or even flinches before the snap, making the defense believe the play has started before it really has.

Fair catch: When a kick or punt returner agrees not to advance the football after catching a kick, with the defense not allowed to tackle or hit the player.

Field goal range: An offense having the ball close enough to the goal post for their kicker to be able to make a field goal.

Flag: The yellow "flag" or marker that officials use to indicate a penalty has been committed during a play.

Fumble: When a ball carrier loses possession of the football during a play, allowing the defense to take possession.

Goal line: The front edge of the end zone going back into the field of play. It is the goal line a ball carrier must pass in order to score a touchdown.

Hail Mary: A long pass normally thrown by the team that is behind at the very end of the half or the game to try to score a touchdown.

Interception: When the defense catches a forward pass thrown by an offensive player.

Line of scrimmage: The place on the field where the football lies at the start of every play.

Live ball: Any time a ball is being advanced or is available to be picked up by either team.

Mismatch: When one team is vastly superior to another or when an offensive player or the defensive player guarding him has a definite advantage over the other. One example could be a fast wide receiver who ends up being defended by a slower defensive lineman because of the defensive scheme of the play called.

NFL Players Association: The labor union that represents the players of the National Football League.

Offense: The team with possession of the football at the start of a play.

Official: Those on the field in charge of keeping the game moving, calling penalties, and understanding the rules.

Offsides: When any part of a defensive player is across the line of the ball placement as the ball is snapped.

Onside kick: When a kickoff is intentionally kicked close to the ground, giving the kicking team a chance to recover the ball and regain possession after it travels at least 10 yards.

Pass route: The direction and angle a pass catcher is running in order to catch a pass and gain yards.

Penalties: Infractions against either a player or coach who violates the rules during a football game.

Pick-six: When the defense catches a pass for an interception and runs all the way into the end zone for a touchdown.

Playbook: A book containing diagrammed football plays that a team uses to strategize for an upcoming opponent.

Play clock: The clock that shows how much time an offense has to run their next play before incurring a delay-of-game penalty.

Pocket: The space an offensive line tries to create around a quarterback for him to try to throw downfield.

Possession: The team snapping and putting the ball in play has "possession." A possession also refers to gaining control of the football and is important in situations such as a receiver successfully catching a pass (gaining control) before going out of bounds or fumbling.

Punt: When a team kicks the ball after failing to get a first down and not kicking a field goal.

Receive: To catch a thrown or kicked football.

Receiver: A player who catches passed or kicked footballs.

Red zone: The offensive team calls reaching the 20-yard line of the defense's territory the red zone, a place where it is always important to score points on each possession.

Replay official: An official who is watching the game and is called upon to make a ruling when coaches challenge a call on the field. They are also allowed to stop the game if they see an injured player, especially one who might have a concussion.

Rush: When a defensive player goes after the quarterback to try to get a sack, or after a kicker to try to block a punt or field goal. Rushing is also a term that is used when a running back is carrying the football on a running play.

Sack: Any time a defensive player tackles the quarterback behind the line of scrimmage, they are credited with a sack; or if two players make the tackle, each is given a half a sack.

Salary cap: The limit on how much money an NFL team can spend on players during a season. The amount of the salary cap is based on how much money the league makes and the rules written into the collective bargaining agreement.

Scoring position: An offense having the ball close enough to the end zone for a touchdown or to the goal post for their kicker to make a field goal.

Slant: A route pattern typically run by the receiver, where the receiver runs up the field a few yards, then cuts 45 degrees to the center of the field.

Snap: The action of the center giving the ball to the quarterback or kick holder, which starts the play.

Special teams: The players who are on the field during any type of kick (kick off, punt, field goal attempt).

Spike: When a quarterback is trying to stop the clock, he will spike the ball into the ground as an incomplete pass. Spikes are also seen after touchdowns when a player will throw the ball hard toward the ground in celebration of the score.

Spot: Where the ball is after a ball carrier is tackled. A referee will "spot" the ball by placing it down and signaling they are ready to start the next play. A "spot foul" is a penalty that is marked off where the penalty took place rather than the original line of scrimmage.

Territory: Each team's "territory" is 50 yards—the half of the football field they are defending for that quarter of the game.

Touchback: When a kick goes into the end zone and the receiving team is given the ball at a certain spot on the field to start their next possession. On kickoffs, the offense starts on the 25-yard line; on punts, it's the 20-yard line.

Touchdown: The act of a ball carrier reaching their opponent's end zone with the football, earning six points for their team.

Training camp: The time of year before the regular season starts when teams assemble, practice, play exhibition games, and decide who is going to be on their roster. This normally takes place in late July and August.

Turnover: Any time a defense takes the ball away from the offense it is called a turnover. A fumble recovery and an interception are the most common forms of a turnover.

Two-point conversion: An optional play by the offense that can be run after a touchdown, which, if successful, gives a team two points.

Two-minute warning: At the end of the second and fourth quarters, the clock will stop with two minutes remaining, giving each team an automatic timeout to set their strategy for the remainder of the quarter.

Wild card: A team that does not win their division but has a good enough record to reach the playoff in their conference is a wild card team. The AFC and NFC have three wild-card teams every season and they can be from any division within the conference.

Zone defense: When a team decides to have their linebackers and secondary players each guard an area of the field rather than a specific offensive player.

RESOURCES

FootballBabble.com
A website for American football novices, created by a novice, covering all aspects of the game.

Operations.NFL.com
A website for NFL fans, created by the NFL, that gives an in-depth look at how the NFL operates and functions at all levels.

ProFootballHoF.com
A website showcasing the history of American football and every NFL Hall of Famer.

Pro-Football-Reference.com
A database containing stats and important information on every NFL player, team, and coach throughout history.

REFERENCES

BOOKS

Ellenport, Craig. *NFL 100: The Greatest Moments of the NFL's Century.* Chicago: Triumph Books, 2019.

Holloway, Jerrett. *Football for Kids: Learn the Basics & Play the Game.* Emeryville, CA: Rockridge Press, 2021.

WEB

"Football 101: How a quarterback 'reads' a defense (aka Defensive coverage schemes)," by Kevin Nogle. ThePhinsider .com/2016/6/27/12039106/football-101-defensive-cover -schemes-aka-how-a-quarterback-reads-a-defense.

NFL.com. "Amazon Prime Video to be exclusive 'TNF' home starting in 2022." May 3, 2021. NFL.com/news/amazon-prime-video -to-be-exclusive-tnf-home-starting-in-2022.

NFL Football Operations. "NFL Video Rulebook: Down by Contact." Accessed October 15, 2021. Operations.NFL.com/the-rules /nfl-video-rulebook/down-by-contact.

NFL Football Operations. "NFL Video Rulebook: Play Clock." Accessed October 15, 2021. Operations.NFL.com/the-rules /nfl-video-rulebook/play-clock.

NFL Football Operations. "2021 Official Playing Rules of the National Football League." Accessed October 15, 2021. Operations.NFL.com/media/5427/2021-nfl-rulebook.pdf.

INDEX

ACKNOWLEDGEMENTS

JERRETT: I would like to thank my co-author, Rafael Thomas, for helping me write this book. Also, I would like to thank Rebecca Markley who helped edit the book and the entire Callisto Media team for providing support and presenting the opportunity to write this book.

RAFAEL: I would like to thank Jerrett Holloway for giving me a chance to write for his website, TooAthletic.com, and allowing me to take one of the most interesting and exciting rides of my life. I am looking forward to many more opportunities with him and (hopefully) with Callisto Media. Thank you also to Paul Whyte for helping me during some dark and difficult times, and my sisters who are always out there inspiring me to do better every day and make you proud. I would also like to thank all the visitors of TooAthletic.com who challenge me to be a better, more insightful writer every day.

ABOUT THE AUTHORS

Jerrett Holloway is the founder of and a contributing writer for TooAthletic.com. Jerrett grew up in the Philadelphia area and is a fan of the Philadelphia Eagles. However, his favorite athlete is Tom Brady.

Rafael Thomas is a born-and-raised New Yorker and a long-suffering Mets and Jets fan, and first started writing about sports professionally for TooAthletic.com. Rafael is also a bookkeeper, allowing him to analyze sports in a unique way. Rafael has two younger sisters, Jessica and Isabella, who he hopes will see this book, smile, and be proud of their big brother.

Printed in the USA
CPSIA information can be obtained
at www.ICGtesting.com
CBHW040309050324
4972CB00013B/110